Banana Ball

The Unbelievably True Story
of the Savannah Bananas

JESSE COLE

with Don Yaeger

DUTTON

DUTTON

An imprint of Penguin Random House LLC
penguinrandomhouse.com

Copyright © 2023 by Jesse Cole
Penguin Random House supports copyright. Copyright fuels creativity, encourages
diverse voices, promotes free speech, and creates a vibrant culture. Thank you for
buying an authorized edition of this book and for complying with copyright laws
by not reproducing, scanning, or distributing any part of it in any form without
permission. You are supporting writers and allowing Penguin Random House to
continue to publish books for every reader.

DUTTON and the D colophon are registered trademarks
of Penguin Random House LLC.

LIBRARY OF CONGRESS CATALOGING-IN-PUBLICATION DATA
has been applied for.

ISBN 9780593473412 (hardcover)
ISBN 9780593473436 (ebook)

Printed in the United States of America
1st Printing

While the author has made every effort to provide accurate telephone numbers, internet
addresses, and other contact information at the time of publication, neither the publisher
nor the author assumes any responsibility for errors or for changes that occur after
publication. Further, the publisher does not have any control over and does not assume
any responsibility for author or third-party websites or their content.

To my dad, who taught me to "swing hard in case you hit it,"

and to future Banana Ballers for bringing joy to the game

and making baseball fun

Contents

Banana Ball

Foreword

I wasn't ready for the energy coming from the other end of the line when Jesse Cole called me in late 2021. Jesse and the Savanah Bananas were embarking on a tour he was sure was going to serve as a true coming-out party for what was already, in my opinion, the most interesting sporting/entertainment organization in America, and I wanted to learn more.

The team was heading out to stadiums throughout the Southeast and Midwest during the spring of 2022, bringing the world—and themselves—proof that the buying public was ready for a fresh take on "America's pastime." His plan sounded simple: Take the best of baseball and make it better, and take what drives everyone crazy—the long games; the corporate, even inaccessible, vibe—and make it intimate and wildly fan-friendly. Every decision, every stunt, every *concession*: it was all about being Fans First.

Jesse had introduced the idea of baseball played by new rules to the world earlier that year during a One-City World Tour in Mobile, Alabama, and I had followed the experience from afar, mostly through his team's amazing social media accounts. The ideas the Bananas added to the game—a fan can catch a foul ball and register an out; a walk actually becomes a sprint when the batter takes off after the fourth errant pitch—were the kinds of uber-creative twists on a sport that has lost touch with a young generation.

But as a longtime *Sports Illustrated* writer and author, and a baseball nut for whom the game had gone a bit stale, I'll confess I was skeptical—all the energy the Bananas showed on TikTok and Instagram couldn't possibly be true to life. I was sure social media added ten times the appearance of fun to the games, the same way a television camera adds ten pounds. Baseball was an unmovable, unfixable thing, so bound by rules and traditions, it was unimprovable. And while I didn't think that was necessarily a good thing, it is what I believed was true.

Then came the invitation from Jesse: Come experience what we're doing. See it for your skeptical self.

The word *unicorn* is used too often, in my opinion. But in my thirty-plus years of covering the worlds of sports and business, it was the only word I could apply to Jesse. The invitation had barely crossed his lips when I jumped at the opportunity to go watch a game and understand the current of fan love that it tapped into. Almost immediately I started wondering if there might be a book in the telling of this effort. That first game pushed me over the top! I wanted to capture that explosion of creative energy and help others appreciate the story behind the man and his family who are dedicated to delivering it every night. His energy pulled me in; he doesn't just bend the rules out of irreverence, but out of true love of the game, and because his creative well is deep. Whatever we think of as convention, he's going to try doing the opposite. But it's his constant willingness to adapt and improve the show he delivered that made me feel like I was in the presence of a modern-day Walt Disney.

After Jesse agreed a book would add to the overall growth of the movement he was hoping to create, I and my writing team attended every Banana Ball–rules game that year. And I was right: social media *didn't* accurately cover the experience of being there. Being there was *even* zanier, wilder, more unpredictable, and more pure fun than anything I'd ever seen on any field. I experienced the highs and the lows, the drama and the dramatic, and I watched as Jesse's band of creatives thrilled tens of thousands of fans, setting up a future that only the wildest imagination (read: Jesse Cole) could paint.

On several of these road trips, I brought my young-teen children along. When the first game ended, I noticed that my son, Will, hadn't been on his phone once during the two hours. With a big smile on his face, he said, "Dad, please don't take me to a regular baseball game ever again." In many ways, I'm with him!

The Bananas are just crossing the starting line, with Jesse out front in that yellow tux. Where they go—and as they go—they'll have me and millions more there with them!

Don Yeager
January 2023

Introduction

This is not a memoir.

But here's the thing. Ever since I had the vision of re-creating baseball, ever since my wife, Emily, and I formed the Savannah Bananas, I've gotten a fair amount of attention. And I don't think it's only because I own seven yellow tuxedos (complete with a matching top hat). Admittedly, I have put myself out there for any opportunity to tell our story. Maybe it's because we're doing something so different that people can't look away, almost like they want to meet us and investigate.

This is not a book about your grandpa's favorite pastime. This is not about baseball. This is about the greatest show in sports. This is about Banana Ball and how it got started. In order to understand how it came to be, you have to understand how I came to be as well. And then, at least if you get to the end and you think Banana Ball is the craziest thing you've ever heard of, you have a name you can blame for the insanity.

My name is Jesse Cole. This is the story of the lessons I learned early and how they played into the lessons that I hope I continue to learn today.

OK, if you're stuck on wordplay, call it a memoir if you insist. It does include a lot of stuff about my childhood, my amateur baseball career, my hopes, my dreams, the tremendous team at my side, how Emily made me the luckiest man alive when she agreed to be my wife (on a ball field, of course), and how the direction of our life together was somehow steered toward the Bananas.

That sounds like a traditional memoir.

But I prefer to say this book is about a full-fledged movement, maybe even a revolution.

When we came up with the name Savannah Bananas—seriously, who names a baseball team after a fruit?—the local fans almost rode us out of town. But from the beginning, with our brand of flair and showmanship, with a fun-filled, fast-paced version of the game that we call Banana Ball, we've always had one priority.

You.

The fans.

Our slogan—now, then, and forever—is simple: *Fans First. Entertain Always.*

When we started the Bananas, Emily and I were deeply in debt from launching our team. We were sleeping on an air mattress, living in a three-hundred-square-foot studio, eating ramen noodles and Hot Pockets. Yeah, our prospects didn't look so good. But I guess far greater odds have been overcome. Back then, all we had was family, a few of our nonskeptical friends, and each other—along with a persistent belief that if we somehow got people to our ballpark, they would have more fun than they had ever dreamed possible.

Our team endured and innovated to the point where the Bananas have played to nearly a decade's worth of sold-out crowds and attracted more social media followers than any major-league team. The Bananas were the subject of a five-part ESPN documentary. We executed a thirty-three-city World Tour—some fans followed us around, sort of like the Grateful Dead's Deadheads—and then we planned to bring Banana Ball into MLB stadiums.

We're different. Let me give you an example.

Baseball doesn't have a clock. That's part of its charm, right? The game is timeless. At least that's what we've been told for the last century or so.

Play ball!

That's what you always hear in baseball. Everybody knows that one. We say it, too. But a few seconds later, before our first pitch, we also say this:

Start the clock!

We have a clock, and our games top out at two hours. We don't allow bunts. Batters can steal first base. And if a fan catches a foul ball in the stands, it's an out. Crazy, right?

Remember when *Moneyball* came out? If you didn't read the book, you probably saw the movie. It was interesting because it challenged traditional baseball tactics, specifically the way teams viewed and scouted players. It showed how a team with no money could compete with the richest teams in baseball by picking out subtle winning qualities of players who had been passed over or labeled as has-beens.

For years, the baseball standings practically ran parallel to the payrolls. Small-market teams had no shot at all. Then some of them found an edge, and it was so contradictory to baseball's structure. And that fascinated fans. The little guys could actually win? How? That shouldn't work. Why did it work?

In their own way, the Bananas are accomplishing something similar. We are changing the game and growing fans faster than all the major-league baseball teams combined. You see fans proudly wearing their Bananas gear at MLB games. They usually are greeted by cheers. Our social media presence has exploded. We are putting fun and fans first—not stats, not analytics, not data, and not dollars.

We are challenging the traditional view that it's all about wins and losses and the ultimate goal of putting together a winning team. Yes, we want to win and play well, but we're putting together the most *fun* team in baseball. My argument always has been that if you assemble the most fun group and create a great environment, you'll have the largest and most loyal fan base. You'll also win quite often.

We still hear the contradictory view: according to conventional thinking, the Bananas *shouldn't* work. We never had big dollars. We never had an investor from the outside. And we've primarily played in a home ballpark with a capacity of four thousand—going up to ten thousand or so at stadiums during our World Tour. But with our attention to social media, we have reached *millions*.

I'm the front man for this baseball revolution. Some people call me the ringmaster. You *should* know Emily, but probably don't, because she's always in the background, smoothing out my craziness with her voice of reason, handling thankless details, and, most important, keeping our family safe and happy in her loving embrace. You *need* to know our tireless staff, the greatest bunch of hardworking, creatively zany, problem-solving, fun-loving people in the history of people. They are fueled by caffeine, sarcasm, and imagination. I love their nonstop ideas and their willingness to challenge traditional beliefs.

So why do the Bananas work? In a world filled with entertainment options and competition for the sports dollar, what is our hook?

From the minute you arrive—I mean, when your car door actually opens and you approach our stadium—we are dedicated to your entertainment. Dead time? Dirty words. We want you engaged, smiling, and laughing—with your head practically on a swivel, not knowing where to turn next—and that includes after the game, when all the players gather in front of the stadium to sign autographs, take pictures, and dance with the fans.

We have some of the world's greatest baseball entertainers—a player who pitches and hits on stilts; a player who comes to the plate with his bat on fire; a player who delivers pitches behind his back, between his legs, or after a somersault; a player who hits while blindfolded, plus the fastest man in baseball—and all of them are constantly singing, dancing, doing backflips, or maybe even running into the stands to give you a high five.

In just our first year of the Banana Ball World Tour, we have been joined on the field by so many former major-league all-stars who have played for the Bananas. Guys like Bill Lee, who has probably played more baseball in more leagues than anybody in the history of the planet. He found his home—and some of his greatest success—at seventy-five years young, with the Bananas. Guys like Jake Peavy, Jonathan Papelbon, Eric Byrnes, Josh Reddick, and Jonny Gomes—iconic major leaguers, award winners, and now some of our most devoted ambassadors, after they experienced the joy of playing Banana Ball.

In many MLB circles, the Bananas have gone from a faraway curiosity to a front-burner issue. Behind closed doors in the executive suites, they're wondering: *What's their secret?* I know they're thinking this because more and more they are actually calling and asking this. It's still surreal to talk to these huge brands and give them insight and advice.

But it's really not a secret at all. It's *Fans First. Entertain Always.*

I grew up in the Boston area. My dad used to take me to Red Sox games at Fenway Park. When I was five, I was a batboy and had my picture taken with some Red Sox players. When I was twenty, I pitched at Fenway as part of a college summer-league all-star team.

When I was a kid, I dreamed of getting drafted by the Red Sox. I visualized the phone call from the Red Sox and my celebration after getting the news. For the last few years, my dream has evolved to having the Bananas play at a sold-out Fenway Park.

Well, that dream could become reality.

The Red Sox were one of the MLB teams that noted how the Bananas were attracting a new generation of baseball fans. So in September 2022, they brought us to Fenway and asked lots of questions about our approach and execution.

As I walked up Fenway's ramp and stared out at the Green Monster, it was a whole different view from those I'd had when I made that walk as a kid. I wasn't trying to be romantic about it, but I just looked around and took it all in. My dad was also there, and he looked around with a puzzled expression, almost like, *What is happening here?* I couldn't walk two feet without somebody stopping me to say hello or ask me to pose for a picture.

I visualized thirty-five thousand fans at Fenway—all of them wearing banana costumes. The whole ballpark looked so much smaller to me, so everything seemed more doable, more attainable. It felt like, *Yeah, we can do this.* We talked with the Red Sox staff about the parade we would stage outside the ballpark—our marching band; players firing off Roman candles, dancing in the streets. You soon realize that the Bananas are about so much more than a baseball game.

As one of the Red Sox officials said, "This will be like an actual circus coming to our ballpark."

Yeah.

Of course. What else would you expect?

I don't believe we've even scratched the surface yet with the Savannah Bananas. We're barely in the first inning. But to already have that kind of acceptance from MLB—and to know that there are cities all over America and the world that desperately want to host our games—it pretty much blows my mind.

I could say that where the Bananas are now is a total reflection of our vision and plans for what we wanted the Bananas to become. But I think it's more indicative of the people who showed up and spoke out, letting everyone know they crave a fan experience that makes them feel like a kid again.

It's one heck of a story already, and I'm ready to give you a peek behind the curtain, where we can experience all the exhilaration and some of the heartbreak that got us here. That's right . . . heartbreak. We have been perceived as failures and criticized pretty harshly. We have faced challenges and overcome adversity. But even through all of that, we never stopped believing in what the Bananas could be.

Our story isn't perfect, but I think we're headed in the right direction. As you see how we've grown, you'll get a flavor for what makes us tick. You'll get a heaping helping of all-out craziness, and you'll sense the long-term satisfaction that comes only when a bunch of good people are dedicated to a cause they believe in. I'll say it again: We've only just begun.

Banana Ball!

Are you ready for this?

Start the clock!

Chapter One

The Beginning

This is a love story, and it starts in the comfortable three-bedroom Massachusetts home I shared with my father. I was a rail-thin nine-year-old boy and, late every afternoon, my ball cap on straight and a baseball held firmly in hand, I stared at the doorknob of the front door. I waited anxiously for it to turn, signaling Dad's return home from work.

My first love was playing baseball with my dad. It didn't matter how I was doing in school, whether my friends were around, or how boring my day had been. He was there for me every single day. I could count on my dad . . . and I could count on baseball.

I still can.

In 2015, my wife and I started a college summer-league team. We sold out every game from the beginning. We won championships. For many people, that would have been enough.

Somewhere along the way, baseball had become so painful to watch that even the announcers seemed exhausted from its plodding pace. Why not, Emily and I felt, try something different? We wanted to jazz up the game and put fans on the edge of their seats—and make them smile.

Our baseball team, we quickly learned, seemed like a grass-roots movement, and it was also our wake-up call. Slumbering baseball fans craved change to the game—at least the fans who still cared—and the Bananas somehow struck a nerve.

Now we're an elite pro team. We're touring the country and, one day, the world. We have our own Banana Ball rules, where we get rid of the game's laborious moments and give fans more of what they really want—fast-paced excitement and things they never imagined seeing on a baseball field. We think more and more talented players will want to go bananas because our game gives them a chance to show off their personalities while also creating the kind of fun they enjoyed as kids.

My younger self couldn't have imagined the life I have with the Bananas. I mean, I thought I loved the game. But maybe what I really loved were memories of a carefree time, when the stadium lights flickered on, spikes clickety-clacked on the sidewalk, and the freshly mowed grass was the sweetest smell. Baseball fans still live for that sound the ball makes when it pops into a glove, for the sound of the crowd. When I was a kid, the game made me feel so alive.

But long before I owned seven yellow tuxedos, long before reporters from the *Wall Street Journal* and the *New York Times* shared features on our outrageous entertainment business, long before ESPN produced a five-part documentary on how our baseball revolution came about, I stared at that doorknob. And I waited.

When I was a kid, playing baseball was the only time when everything seemed normal. Some people these days say the Bananas are out to save baseball for the next generation. Maybe that's true. But I know this for sure: baseball saved my childhood.

When I was eight years old in my hometown of Scituate, Massachusetts, my dad brought me into the living room and told me he and my mom were getting a divorce. I didn't understand why people got divorced. Nobody I knew talked about divorce. None of my friends' parents were divorced. In my mind, parents always stayed together, no matter what.

When my dad broke the news, I kept thinking it was my fault. I was not the easiest kid to raise. Years later, my dad told me I was very "opinionated." Maybe I blamed myself for my parents' splitting. I just knew I didn't want to hear about a divorce.

"Dad, what do I need to do?" I said while sitting on the couch. "I don't want this. Just tell me."

"Jesse, it's just not that easy," my dad said solemnly. "You'll understand this better when you get older. We both want what's best for you."

With tears in my eyes, I kept saying, "I'll be better. I'll try. I'll listen. I'll do what you guys say. Please stay together. Please. I'll be better. I promise! Please!"

It wasn't that simple, my dad kept telling me. There were things I couldn't grasp about the demons my mother was battling. I didn't understand about addictions and how they could rip apart a family. I was just a kid who wanted his parents to stay together. I didn't want my life to change in such a scary kind of way.

I didn't want scary; I wanted simple.

When I stared at that doorknob every day, I was minutes away from escaping all my worries. Somebody once wrote that the seams of a baseball formed a lifeline for me and my dad. That is so true. I was all dressed up with somewhere to go. I couldn't wait for my dad to come home from work so I could come back to life.

When the doorknob turned and my dad burst into the house, it didn't matter if he was tired from his job. It didn't matter what he had to do that night. We were headed to the ball field. I felt so happy and free.

Sometimes, a boy rebels against his dad, or the relationship becomes a battle of wills between two stubborn guys. I feel sad when I hear about guys who don't have positive relationships with their fathers or whose relationships grow strained over time. I never had that experience.

Even today, when I get beautiful personal messages from people about the Bananas and how our show affected them, my first thought is usually, *I have to send these to my dad. He would love this.* And he's always like, "Man, this means so much. I never would've imagined this." I know he's proud. That still means everything to me.

I know my dad is proud of the Savannah Bananas, too.

In a way, that's funny. My dad was always big on playing baseball "the right way." And the Bananas break so many of those "rules" that are gospel to baseball purists. Some people won't take anyone or anything seriously unless they're buttoned-up and professional. Well, I have a different perspective about that. I don't believe anybody comes home and says, "Honey, I met the most professional person today. She was just so professional." I don't think we get excited about being professional.

I think we get excited about memorable, unique, fun, and different. If people want to have fun, they must take chances. So we challenge people to embrace the fun. Some people say that's not for them. Well, why not? Give it a try. Loosen that tie. Have some fun. See if it brings more purpose and enjoyment.

Unfortunately, I didn't try to have fun, or make fun, in high school ball or college ball. I took it seriously, and I have regrets about that. I wouldn't trade my baseball-playing days, but I think my approach gradually changed. Now, with the Bananas, life has been beyond anything I could have ever imagined.

One thing has continued, though.

When I was at Wofford College and later, while running the teams in Gastonia, North Carolina, or Savannah, I'd usually work out on the field with my dad. We'd get the music blasting in the stadium. We would do some long throws and some soft toss. We'd either go to the cages or we might hit on the field; then we'd take ground balls.

These days, we don't do it all the time. My dad is now in his seventies. I'm pushing forty, and I've usually got a million things going on with the Bananas. I'm super focused because there are so many details to account for in Bananas games.

But when my dad and I are together at a game, we like to have our own fun. If it's just the two of us on the field, we hit and play catch.

There's a reason why so many men were blindsided by the film *Field of Dreams* when it first came out. They first tried to hold back the tears, then realized there was no shame in showing their emotions. The baseball movie ended up being a love story that ended with a father playing catch with his son.

There's no question that my dad had a major influence on all of my baseball experiences. But beyond that, whatever good qualities I have are because I watched the way he lived his life.

The best example was in 2013, when we learned my dad had two forms of cancer. There was non-Hodgkin's lymphoma outside of his liver, a tumor that was spreading quickly. The doctors found colon cancer as well, so they decided to treat the cancers aggressively.

He was at Beth Israel hospital in Boston, and I was down in

Gastonia. He insisted I stay and told me, "Jesse, just do your thing. I'm going to be fine."

I called my dad every single day. I would say, "Dad, how are you doing?"

And he always said, "Yes, I'm great, I'm great," even when he was actually in the middle of chemo and going through unbelievable pain.

About six months into his treatment, I remember calling and asking, "Dad, how are you?"

And he just said, "I'm good." He didn't say *great*. He said *good*.

I found out he had thrown up the whole night and had been extremely sick. All I could think was, *He said* good, *not* great.

Well, the next day, I called and he told me, "I'm great." Every single day after that, he said *great*. Every single day.

A few months later, when he was in complete remission and the cancer had been defeated, the nurses told me my dad had been the most positive patient they had ever had in the hospital, even though he had gone through more pain, more challenges, and more adversity than just about anybody.

So when people ask me what's the best advice I ever got, I always say it wasn't advice. It was watching my dad every single day, how he dealt with these severe challenges and adversity, and how he coped with his fight against cancer.

Do I have my share of challenges like anybody else? Of course. But after watching what my dad went through and seeing how he handled that, how can I not take on a positive outlook on everything I do?

Yes, if you can't tell already, I'm extremely excited about what we've built with the Bananas and how people all over the world have climbed aboard. Who knows how big Banana Ball can get? Yes, I'm the guy in the yellow tux and top hat, the guy who can't do enough crazy stuff, the guy trying to bring more fun into base-ball. I'm loud and outrageous, some might even say a little "out there."

But you know what? My greatest joy has been that I have got-ten to share all of these experiences with my dad.

I'm still that kid who's staring at the doorknob.

I still want to make my dad proud.

Chapter Two

Scituate, Massachusetts

I grew up in Scituate, Massachusetts, a classic American small town filled with summer cottages, picturesque views, and friendly people. We were on the South Shore, about an hour out of Boston, an hour from Cape Cod, and probably one mile to the Atlantic Ocean. You might call me a beach bum. We went quite often.

Our house was a really comfortable place. It had a pool in the back and about an acre of land for me to play on—and that's a good thing for an only child with a vivid imagination.

Even when I was a kid, though, there were days when I knew things weren't quite right.

From the earliest times I can remember, my mother would sleep in, sometimes all the way until noon. It went on up until when my parents got divorced. My dad would leave a bowl of cereal and a half cup of milk inside the fridge for me, and that was my breakfast. My mother didn't do it because she was sleeping.

Most days, my dad would go to work, my mother would sleep, and I would be all alone. We had this upside-down house, and the kitchen was on the top floor. One time after my dad had left in the morning, when I was probably about three years old, I decided to play in the kitchen sink. I got on a stool and climbed into the sink with all my toys. Then I guess I got bored with that, so I went in the other room to watch TV, but I left the water running full blast.

For about an hour, water poured down the lower cabinets and onto the floors. I had no idea that our house was flooding. Eventually, it started seeping through the ceiling to the first floor. All of a sudden, my mother woke up because the fire alarms and smoke detectors were going off. She called my dad in a panic. My dad told her to get out of the house.

There was three feet of water when the fire trucks finally arrived. My dad came all the way home from work to discover there had never been a fire but that our house was flooded. He was frustrated to say the least.

My dad was the only one making money. He had a big job at Bradlees, where he was the regional manager for that chain of discount department stores in the Northeast. My mother, I guess, was in her own world.

Here's the thing: my mother was and is a really good person. She was loving when she was there and when she was awake. I'm told there were times when she loved cuddling with me or reading me books. I just don't remember much of that because I was so young.

I was responsible as a child. I washed the floors and did the laundry when I was eight years old. I wasn't sure what my mother was actually going through. I'd say it was a strange time frame for me, but it was all I knew.

My dad was a constant and comforting presence in my life. For me, he was it. He was everything.

He obviously had a vision, and he could see two outcomes for me. Either I would be with my mother or I would be with him. I have love for my mother, but we don't talk very much, and she's still struggling with challenges. Had she raised me, I would have led a completely different life, with a completely different outcome.

My dad fought hard and invested heavily in doing whatever was necessary to make sure I was with him. That wasn't for selfish reasons. Actually, it was selfless. My parents shared custody, but my dad was the one who raised me, even though raising a child as a single parent was difficult. He did what was best for his son, juggling his own life and career.

There were a few years when it was just my dad and me. He was always scrambling to make sure I had some form of after-school care. At one point there were different sitters. Then, there was an after-school program that I didn't like at all. Sometimes I would go to a friend's house and their mother would help with homework and occasional meals. It was a constant struggle to get the right people in place. By the time I reached fourth grade or so, every day was a challenge. For a while, it seemed like my head was spinning because I never knew where I'd spend the time after school.

Things got a lot easier when my dad began a relationship. It was great for him, and a few years later, my dad was fortunate enough to remarry. We all love Diane. She has been great for my dad. I also got a stepbrother out of the deal—Diane's son, Andrew—so my teenage years didn't feel so lonely. We were both about fourteen when they got married. It was a perfect match— two rambunctious boys, the same age—and we had a lot of laughs.

I was excited when my dad and Diane told us they were getting married. I felt like we had a complete family. When they married on Clearwater Beach in 1999, it was just them, Andrew and me, Diane's mother, and the justice of the peace. That's when our lives grew more stable.

It was probably a bigger adjustment for Andrew, because he and Diane moved into our house in Scituate, but it didn't take him long to warm up to it because he had been hanging out there before.

It was vastly different from the time immediately following my parents' divorce. There had been a lot of loneliness. I really had friends only through baseball. I don't remember a lot of kids hanging around my house or having that crazy pack of kids you see roaming around some neighborhoods.

Summers had been tough. My dad would come home from work and say, "Jesse, what did you do today?"

And I would say, "Well, I rode my bike to Alex's house." He was happy to hear that. But the truth was, I actually never rode my bike to Alex's house. I just didn't want to tell him that I had spent the day alone. I wasn't an antisocial person. There just weren't any other kids around. I felt lost.

Things changed with my new brother, and with baseball. When I got to high school, I always had a good base of friends. And obviously, with what has happened in my life with the Bananas and our business, I now constantly interact with people. But I remember what it's like to be lonely.

That's why it was so important to make my dad proud. When I got good grades or my dad got a nice report from teachers, he would put a stack of baseball cards on my desk with a note that said something like, "Good job! Just keep up the good work."

When I was ten or eleven, when I started hitting home runs over the fence, my dad offered me money for that. Those were cool moments. I always knew he was watching me.

My dad's name is Kerry Cole. He was born in New York, and then his family moved around. When my dad was nine, they settled in Old Saybrook, Connecticut, which is right on the mouth of the Connecticut River and Long Island Sound. His father—my grandfather—had worked for Woolworth Co., but he opened his own five-and-dime when they got to Old Saybrook.

My dad always told me that I'm a lot like my grandfather: fearless and absolutely not afraid to take chances. I regret not having known my grandfather, because he died in 1984, the year I was born. There are a few pictures of my grandfather holding me when I was a baby, but that's about it.

My dad was probably the best athlete in his town. While he was winning multiple awards, my grandfather was being recruited by several retail chains. He finally gave in, sold the five-and-dime, and went to work for Bradlees. But he didn't want to disrupt my dad's three-sport athletic career at Old Saybrook, so he commuted from Connecticut to Boston, which was two hours, fifteen minutes one way. My grandfather didn't want to make my dad move, because it would've disrupted his senior year. Instead, my grandfather made the sacrifice to spend hours in the car on a regular basis for the sake of his son. With that as an example, it's not hard to realize why my dad had the instinct to sacrifice so much for me and why I would one day make some of the same parental choices.

My dad went to a junior college but then decided to begin his career in retail and eventually landed at Bradlees, too. Maybe I had the fearlessness of my grandfather, but I definitely inherited a fierce work ethic from my dad. My dad set a great example. He lives up to his responsibilities, deals with adversity, and doesn't make excuses. I try to emulate all those characteristics.

It wasn't perfect for him. My dad was surrounded by a lot of smart people in a very competitive business. Hard work was his path to success. He also treated people right. He was fair but firm and the kind of guy who was deeply respected. I looked up to my dad and loved spending time with him.

And as you might imagine, we started with baseball pretty early. My dad had these little white balls—we called them "rag balls"—that were made from newspaper pages rolled up in tape. That made them softer than baseballs, so when we played inside the house, we used them to prevent us from breaking things. Well, of course, we got carried away. Once I started swinging the bat, we lost a few lamps to the baseball cause.

My dad was big on positive reinforcement. I always remember him being accessible and encouraging. That was so important during my early stages of baseball. Whatever else I did—whether it was music, soccer, basketball, or track—he was the same way. But he also expected my maximum effort, so I worked my butt off, trying to be the best I could be.

Some kids have dads who work all the time. They grow up and feel like they never fully experience their father. I was so lucky to have the childhood I did. My dad and I had such fun together. I could always be myself and show him my sense of humor. We laughed a lot together.

I've seen dads who force their kids into sports and live vicariously through their games. They push for scholarships—or maybe even making the majors—before their kids are physically mature. That can drive the fun right out of the game. My dad was very laid-back. It was my idea to do baseball workouts. He went along with it immediately, but I took the lead—my dad didn't push me. He never needed to do that. For my part, I was extremely determined to work on my skills and become a better baseball player.

At age ten, I started hitting home runs over the fence. No other ten-year-old in Scituate was doing that. I played on our state's best Amateur Athletic Union (AAU) team and began thinking that potentially I could become one of the better players in Massachusetts.

Our AAU team had thirteen guys who ultimately played Division I baseball—a ridiculous number. We traveled all over the place and played against several guys who wound up in the major leagues, such as Zack Greinke and Scott Kazmir.

Another huge turning point for me was this place called the South Shore Baseball Club, where you could practice baseball indoors. A complete club rat, I was there all the time. The organization was an important part of my development, and eventually my dad left his retail career and purchased part of the baseball club when I was twelve. He became a partner to Frank Niles, one of the best baseball people I have ever known. That gave me access to everything I needed.

It might sound like I became one of those kids who had baseball drilled into them. Not really. Everything was about fun.

Our AAU team marched in from left field like army soldiers, which looked ridiculous, but we loved it. I remember my dad getting a big old boom box, and we played music during practice. That might not seem like a big deal, but those are the things I remember, even more than the games where I hit three home runs or pitched a no-hitter. Those were nice, but I mostly remember the fun.

Maybe that explains why the Savannah Bananas work so well. Even back then, I liked the fun.

When I was away playing for Wofford College in South Carolina, my dad and I stayed in close contact. He's still the first person I call if I'm stuck on a big decision or need advice. He has been a voice of reason with the Bananas, and I love to bounce things off him, whether it's what's going on with the business, our staff, or anything really.

Back when I played catch with my dad in the backyard, or played Little League ball, or became a teenage prospect, or received a college scholarship, I figured it was all part of how I'd have a chance to achieve my biggest dream. Maybe I'd wind up in the major leagues. I'd visualize getting drafted—actually breathlessly rehearsing the big moment, to tell the truth—and playing at Fenway Park for my favorite team, the Boston Red Sox.

That was every kid's dream, right? It was something I constantly imagined.

My childhood years had a dominant theme: baseball was my life.

And baseball was a huge part of my bond with my father. But amid all of those dreams I had for so many years, I never imagined the kind of life where we could work together on finding a new way to play the game that we both loved.

Chapter Three

The Love of the Game

When someone lives in a place like Scituate, Massachusetts, and wants to become a big-time baseball player, there are some realities that they've got to face eventually. The sandbox you're playing in is different from those that kids have in Florida or Texas or California. It just is.

I was considered one of the best players in Massachusetts, probably one of the top five pitchers in the state. Did I want to get drafted and play professional baseball? Heck yeah! But as players get older, they start to realize the quality of players from around the country, especially where there's warmer weather and year-round play. The competition is intense, almost cutthroat at times. Getting to the top requires talent, of course, but ballplayers also need the right timing, good health, and some luck as well.

Yes, the guy who can now be seen in the yellow tux and top hat, the guy who dances on top of the dugout, the one who constantly wants to push baseball out of its comfort zone, was once a hard-bitten ballplayer himself.

Had I not gotten hurt, maybe I would've gotten a shot to pitch in somebody's organization. But I know that would have been a hard, hard road. The odds of making it would have been very slim. But I never had that chance. The torn-labrum injury I suffered in college that ended my life as a baseball player set me on the path to where I am today, with the Savannah Bananas. I believe things happen for a reason.

I am living my purpose, and I'm totally excited about what the Bananas can do for the future of baseball. I have very few regrets.

But me *playing* baseball? Oh my gosh, I miss it in the worst way. To do something that you love so much, to have the camaraderie with teammates and the ability to win big games—it really was the highlight of my young life.

I was like any sports-loving kid in the 1990s. I had my heroes. In basketball, it was Larry Bird. In hockey, there was obviously Wayne Gretzky. In baseball, it was hard to miss Ken Griffey Jr. There were numerous times where I turned my cap backward, like Griffey, and competed in a Wiffle ball home run derby with my friends.

I loved the guys who did things differently. The flair and excitement got me going. I liked to mimic unique batting stances and pitching windups. I got down in that scrunched-up Phil Plantier batting stance. I copied Nomar Garciaparra, one of my Red Sox favorites. I stepped out of the box and shifted around my batting gloves like Nomar did. I envisioned being part of the Red Sox pitching rotation. I pretended I was Hideo Nomo, when he was with the Dodgers, and lifted my arms up high and mimicked his distinctive windup. I actually did it a few times in games with a two-strike count. I'd tell my catcher in advance it was coming so he wouldn't be shocked; then I'd go into my Hideo Nomo routine.

At that stage in my life, I didn't just enjoy the game—I loved the players who made the game fun to watch. Since then, the game has changed. It's lost some of its flair. Remember 1998, when Mark McGwire and Sammy Sosa had their home run chase? Man, I loved how Sosa did his big hop after his homers. Here's what I think happened: If players tried distinctive things in the minor leagues, they were discouraged. Coaches probably told them, "Simplify, simplify, simplify. You don't need that extra stuff. Just get in the box and use your tools." To an extent, that makes sense. But something gets lost along the way—it takes away the uniqueness and individuality of the players.

People always ask me now: "What kind of player were you?" "How good of a pitcher were you?" It's not something I dwell on these days. But here's my scouting report:

I wasn't nice and fluid and easy with the ball. It didn't float out of my hand at ninety-five miles an hour. I was a max-effort guy, going hard on every pitch, showing the tension in my face, sort of like the way Pedro Martinez looked on the mound (although I certainly can't compare myself to Pedro).

My dad always said when I crossed the lines, it was all business. He said I had a presence from a young age. As much as I was having *fun*, I wasn't out there to play around. There was always a purpose. He called me a "wicked competitor." How's that for a Boston-style compliment? Thanks, Dad!

My dad was an awesome baseball father because he had a realistic perspective. He kept his expectations in check. He let my actions and motivations dictate where this baseball thing was going.

I think we both realized there were possibilities when my body started growing and scouts showed interest. They said I had a plus slider (if it's above average in baseball, it is described as "plus") and my changeup kept getting better. I threw those pitches anywhere in the count with great command. I didn't really walk too many guys.

My velocity wasn't necessarily what they wanted, even though I was consistently in the high eighties, maybe touching ninety, ninety-one, or ninety-two at times. Nowadays, if a player is not consistently in the nineties and touching the high nineties, they're not going to give him much of a look. I was effective because of my slider and changeup. I know there were a few scouts who really liked my approach.

Just the *possibility* of someone wanting me, I think that's what I hoped for. I was recruited by college coaches, and professional scouts gave me feedback. I got to live that dream, at least for a while. And living that dream—sensing possibility, having that goal—is a way of being I never forgot.

When I was five years old, my dad always told me, "Swing hard in case you hit it." Everybody laughed, but I took that to heart. I swung hard—always—and played hard. That was my mindset. I swung *so hard* as a kid. Hey, I swung and missed a lot. But when I connected, I made pretty good contact.

My childhood might have been the last generation when doing more than one sport was widely considered a good thing. Baseball was always my number one, but I enjoyed soccer and really loved basketball, too. I had a little basketball hoop inside my room, and I wore that out. I read Larry Bird's book *Drive*, and I really admired him. Of course I loved the Celtics, the Bruins, and all the Boston teams. My dad took me to a lot of Red Sox games, and by now we've probably been in every crack and crevice of Fenway Park. Because my dad was high up at Bradlees and it was a billion-dollar company, it was a sponsor of the Red Sox.

I think it's great for kids to play a variety of sports. Between basketball and soccer and track and cross-country, I got a good sampling. But baseball was where I excelled. And I was lucky to have the right coach early.

At age ten, I started playing AAU ball for the best team in Massachusetts, but my dad didn't even know what an AAU team was until Frank Niles, the guy who founded the South Shore Baseball Club, told him about a tryout. There were kids from all over New England, a tremendous amount of talent, but I made the team and saw a ton of great competition.

The thing I'll always remember about Frank was how he made baseball and being at the South Shore club fun. If there was a rainy day, we'd play dodgeball in the gym. I'd get excited for the rainy days. We'd have "instant-cash trivia" on Tuesdays, where he'd give us $1 and $2 questions; Popsicle challenges; coaches' hitting challenges—the sky was the limit.

Scrub was my favorite game. The game would start with four hitters and the other thirteen or so guys would play in the field. If a player got out on a ground ball or a strikeout, he'd go to right field. If someone flied out, he'd switch with the next guy, but his group kept hitting. It was so fun and competitive. It moved fast. Sort of like Banana Ball!

Frank taught me a valuable lesson when I was fifteen and our AAU team went to the national tournament. For most of the season, I didn't even play. He sat me the entire year. By that time, I was playing varsity high school ball. I was starting ahead of some juniors and seniors. Some parents were even wondering what was going on. I couldn't crack the AAU lineup?

When something happened on the field, Frank always turned to me and the other bench players to say, "Guys, this is what happened here. Here's what they could have done. Here's what they should have done. This is how we get better."

I learned more about baseball that summer than at any other time in my life. He coached us hard on the bench so we would learn. When we went to the national tournament, if somebody wasn't playing well or was making mistakes, Frank would put me in. One game, I got three hits. I played the rest of the tournament and hit about .400. I knew what to do because Frank had taught me . . . while I was sitting on the bench!

I'm in that role now with the Bananas. I might be in the dugout during games and see something we could do for more entertainment. And I'll turn to a player or an intern and describe it. I look at it through a different lens—not necessarily coaching baseball but coaching the organization—and I'm trying to teach. I'm constantly looking at our games and examining everything happening around me, so we can improve and stay fresh. I want everyone to stay alert. I guess that's my way of coaching today.

Little things mean a lot in baseball. I figured that out early on because the game became much more than a pastime to me. It was my way of life. I spent a lot of time at the baseball club, but it's not like I could live there. So at home, my dad built a mound in the backyard. He also got some old mats from the gym, put them on a wood frame, and designed a strike-zone target. Even when my dad wasn't there, I could throw.

Every night, we'd do soft toss and I would hit those rag balls into mattresses. This was a game we had played inside when I was young, but now we took it outside, and the temperature didn't matter. We would still be out there. We'd always end with a speed toss, where I'd challenge my dad to go faster. When I completed the swing, he tossed another one, and I swung harder and harder. When we finished, I always gave my dad a big high five. The next night, we'd try to do more and break our record.

My dad and I really didn't watch many TV shows together. He certainly didn't play video games with me. But we bonded through baseball.

My first really big baseball moment happened in Little League when I was twelve. That's the Williamsport year, when everyone is gunning for the Little League World Series, so that was our dream. We had a great group, and my dad was the coach. He kept expectations reasonable, and we had lots of fun. But there was a game plan in his approach that none of us appreciated at the time. During those kinds of seasons you play *so* many games. But by making the games fun, he kept us fresh. Once we got into districts, we kept winning and winning and winning and, all of a sudden, found ourselves in the state tournament.

Then everyone in Scituate jumped on the bandwagon. The local newspapers had these big headlines: MISSION IMPOSSIBLE. We were like little celebrities. My dad made T-shirts that read "Williamsport Team." That probably rubbed our opponents the wrong way, but I think he was trying to get us to believe in something we couldn't yet see.

Man, our team was exciting. In one game, we were down 6–0 in the last inning. My dad turned to my teammate Greg Levin and said, "Greg, after you hit a home run here, go warm up so you can pitch." Greg said he had never hit a home run before. My dad told him not to worry; that was in the past. So of course Greg hit a home run. Then I hit a home run. We couldn't be stopped. We scored nine runs to win the game.

The whole thing was such a learning experience. When I

pitched a good game, reporters wanted to talk to me. My dad told me all along this was a team sport, not a bunch of individuals trying to get attention. So in every interview, I just talked about the team. It was never about myself.

If I threw a no-hitter, I talked about the support from my defense. And if I hit a homer, I acted professional and stoic, while trotting around the bases, without craziness or celebrations. My dad always told us that was the right way to play baseball.

How crazy is that? With the Bananas, we're the exact opposite.

But I digress.

We did play outstanding baseball. We cared about one another and made it all about the team. We got all the way to the state finals, then came up short. With so many Little League teams in America, it's statistically overwhelming to even have a shot at reaching Williamsport. We got close. That's a memory we'll have forever.

Even with my early success, one thing became painfully obvious. I was one of the smallest kids on my team. I just didn't grow or put on weight like other boys. And that really started to matter in high school.

I was conscious of my size when we played those AAU national tournaments at age eleven or twelve. Guys threw harder and hit these light-tower homers because they were 160 pounds. I might have tipped the scale at 100 pounds—soaking wet.

My size was an even greater issue because I was playing up to the next age group, so I had to compete and really push myself.

Fortunately, my arm speed developed to the point where I could throw the ball out of the stadium from home plate. My bat speed was very good. I put on a show during batting practice.

But when players get older, their physical size becomes more of a factor. On the big field, it's usually the difference between hitting the ball out and coming up just short on the warning track. The pitchers on my AAU team were throwing in the high eight-ies and low nineties. I could get up to eighty-four at that point—maybe. So I wanted to do something about that.

Everything changed in my junior year of high school. At the start of the school year, I weighed 150 pounds. By the time I got to college, I weighed about 225. That's a pretty drastic jump.

People always want to know about the secret formula for building up your body. It's not really a secret. I started train-ing with a guy named Lorenzo—one of his clients was Steven Tyler of Aerosmith—and I did everything he said because he promised me that if I did, I would gain weight. He promised my dad everything he would suggest would be 100 percent natural and done the right way. Basically I ate, and I exercised. He cau-tioned me that I was going to develop a big gut and would be working out like crazy.

And I did. I woke up to an almond butter sandwich followed by a protein shake, then a full breakfast of lean turkey and eggs for protein. Then it was another almond butter protein shake and a full lunch. After school, another shake, then a full dinner. Fi-nally, one more shake before bed. I started doing more sprint, speed, and power work instead of long-distance running.

Just like he said, I developed a belly. It was unbelievably em-barrassing. But we started shaping it up and working out, and I was up about 30 pounds to 180 in about a month, which sounds crazy and probably unnatural. I changed my eating habits dramatically—with all the shakes and calorie intake—and worked out like a maniac.

Then my pitching velocity jumped up to eighty-seven. I started performing at the showcases and tryouts. At showcases, you are usually selected, then assembled into teams with players from other cities. It's all about showcasing your individual skills instead of performing like a team and trying to win games. The whole purpose is for coaches and scouts to see how you throw, hit, and run. I got up to eighty-nine at the Perfect Game Showcase, which is one of the bigger events for young baseball players. In my junior year, I was hitting big-time home runs, like four hundred feet. Pretty soon the word got out.

The letters started pouring in. The first one was from a Division II school. Then it was the University of Maine, a very good Division I baseball program. When I heard from Boston College, I was blown away. Pete Hughes, who was the head coach at the time, said he wanted me as a two-way guy because he liked my hitting. He also told me that as a freshman, I'd have a chance to pitch against the Boston Red Sox in an exhibition game. And I was like, "Whoa! Whoa!" He was speaking my language!

I paid an official visit to Boston College. Two of the players came in, and Coach Hughes said, "Take care of him."

The two guys looked at me and they were like, "Wow! You must be a pretty good recruit. This doesn't normally happen." So we had a party. They took me to a hockey game. We went all over town.

The next day, I told my dad, "We're going to Boston College! It's definite." The problem was they didn't have much scholarship money. BC had only three full scholarships—total—to be divided up by everyone. They offered me maybe $10,000, which was strong, but it cost $30,000 a year to go there. My dad always told me we needed a full scholarship—or as close to that as we could get through athletics and academics—so it wasn't quite enough.

Then Northeastern, another Boston school, reached out. They sent me a letter that read, "Our search for a starting pitcher and impact player starts and ends with you." They thought I had a big-time slider. Northeastern had a great player named Carlos Peña, who became a major-league all-star with the Tampa Bay Rays. They told me that with my stuff, I'd be out of there in three years because I'd get drafted. They offered a really nice scholarship.

Then Wofford College called, and I went down to South Carolina to check it out. Northeastern and Wofford both kept increasing their offers, like a bidding war, but I eventually ended up choosing Wofford. I was blown away by the weather, which is important in baseball because the cold-weather places are at a disadvantage. Coming from Massachusetts, I was used to playing in the snow, while the kids in Florida and California had year-round sunshine.

Wofford was in a smaller Division I conference, but they played Georgia Tech, Texas Tech, South Carolina, and Clemson— just a tremendous schedule against some of the most talented teams in college baseball. I thought it was a great fit for me.

Pro ball was still a dream, too. I got letters from the Atlanta Braves. I got letters from agents who said they wanted to represent me. The San Francisco Giants wanted to know when I was going to pitch in my senior year. They wanted to come watch. It was a crazy, exciting time.

Scouts came to see me play, but my pitching velocity wasn't consistently high enough to keep me on their board as a prospect. The Giants scouts came to my first game, but they never came back. It just didn't work out the way I had dreamed. I was a right-hander at an average height of six foot one, probably throwing eighty-seven to eighty-nine miles an hour. They wanted guys touching the nineties. I didn't have a great body. I wasn't hugely projectable. That's a phrase that baseball insiders use to describe a player whose physical skills will continue to grow. Of course, all kids have major-league dreams, but there are also the realities.

At Wofford, I had good moments. As of 2022, I was still in the record books for the most innings pitched in one game (nine and two-thirds) and I led the team in strikeouts one season. I had a ten-strikeout game against Niagara. I was Southern Conference player of the week and made the league's all-academic team. I also got ripped in a lot of outings, too. The dominance I displayed in high school didn't show up as often in college. That's usually what happens when a player moves up to a more competitive situation.

They say college should open your mind to new ideas. That happened to me, too. I always thought baseball was my greatest talent and biggest niche. As it turned out, I found something else. All of a sudden, I expressed myself in ways I had never really imagined.

Would you guess, knowing what I do now, that I went from the baseball diamond to the theater stage? It turns out, I was a performer.

Who knew?

Chapter Four

Jesse the Entertainer

There I was, bounding onstage as a giant, high-energy fluffy dog, complete with my costume, a conglomeration of dozens of mopheads hand-dyed bright blue. There were probably about three hundred people in the audience that night. I heard them roaring with laughter. That made me even more animated, more hyperactive, and more willing to give my all in the name of entertainment.

One of my classmates said the role was perfect because I was "like a human version of that Labrador retriever."

I could hear the kids up front buzzing and giggling. This was like getting a fastball down the middle. I saw my opportunity. I wanted to steal the show.

OK, this wasn't exactly what I had envisioned when enrolling at Wofford College. I was there to play baseball—and graduate, of course. I couldn't major in baseball. So I had to major in *something*. But what?

I originally had planned to go into business. Smart move, right? But the adviser told me I had to take calculus, macroeconomics, and microeconomics. That didn't sound like business to me. I couldn't see myself learning calculus.

I was going to play baseball, so I had to declare something. But I pretty much wasn't interested in anything. Then I noticed humanities. What was that?

"We've actually never had anyone do a humanities major," the adviser said.

Never?

Hmmm. Tell me more.

I don't actually know how rare it was at Wofford, but the adviser made it sound like majoring in humanities was unprecedented. I liked what I heard. They said I would basically design my own major. They asked what I wanted to study. I said I was fascinated by how to become a great leader. I came up with an idea to study history, government, sports, and business leadership. They went for it.

But it was a lot. I had to do a full-length film, a dissertation speech, and a long research paper. It was independent studies reading, and it concentrated on three different disciplines. I chose theater as one of them.

Why theater? I don't know—it seemed interesting. There were a ton of improv classes. I'm a natural ham, so I thought, *OK, I'll try that.* But then I had to take a new course called Theater for Youth.

When I showed up, I was a fish out of water—in more ways than one. I was strong, muscular, 225 pounds, an athlete. I was the only athlete among a bunch of theater kids. They were all best friends because they had been doing this since they started college. And I was this new kid who didn't know anybody.

But I wasn't a total lost cause. Actually, it wasn't my first rodeo when it came to performing. Back at Scituate High School, my friends and I were known for making movies. Seriously. We made movies all the time, and they were hilarious.

We were a bunch of fun-loving kids, that's for sure. It started when I took a mandatory public-speaking class. It might sound crazy now, but I didn't want to do any speaking because I was scared of that.

In an ongoing theme in my life, I decided to challenge the way things were done. I told the teacher, "There's this thing out now called iMovie. What if, instead of speaking, we do these fully produced and edited videos that we can show? I think that will actually make more of an impact than some of our speeches."

Somehow, I convinced her. She said OK.

Bottom line: I did an entire high school public-speaking class *without giving one speech.* The teacher was determined to not let us get away with anything. She told us, "You're going to have higher expectations put upon yourself. I'm going to be tougher on your grades, and you've got to find a way to make it work."

So I got together with my buddies and said, "Look, we've got to do this right. We've got to make some *great* movies." We made videos that were ridiculously funny—at least in our minds.

We were an incredibly creative group of guys. One of my best friends was Ben Ouellette, who now works as a video and photography producer for an electric truck company in California. He used to work with Arnold Worldwide, a huge firm, and handled accounts like Progressive and Jack Daniel's.

"We were a bunch of guys who enjoyed being around each other and making everyone laugh," Ben said as he recalled our high school group. "Jesse could take the seed of a creative idea, get a lot of confidence with it, and push the boundaries."

The group also included Doug Emmett, who went to New

York University and is now a big-time film and television producer in Los Angeles. It's cool that Doug still remembers our movies.

"When we made those movies, Jesse was just this bundle of energy, like a live-wire ton of energy," Doug said about me as he reminisced about the old days. "He did everything with enthusiasm. He's a natural-born performer, and he loved dressing up to assume different characters. He had a natural spontaneity and impulsivity—kind of intoxicating, really—that you just don't see in many people. He set the pace for all of us."

I guess I was the front man. Whenever we had to do a paper or presentation, I went to the teacher and asked, "What if we made a movie on it?" And a lot of the teachers allowed it. I mean, we were good students, top of our class. We did well in school, so they gave us an opportunity. We performed a lot of shenanigans and high jinks, but we never got called down to the office. We were the good kids doing the shenanigans.

So with that kind of high school background, you'd think getting up onstage in college would be easy for somebody like me, right? Yeah, not exactly. I was scared. I felt completely out of my element. At least I felt that way at first.

Matt Giles, one of the most experienced students in that class, doesn't remember it like that.

"He walked into our room, the baseball player, and it was impossible to not notice his level of energy," Matt said as he recalled my entrance. "We had a lot of interesting and exciting artists, but Jesse walks in, and he's the only person you can look at."

Matt was a serious theater student, and he's now an artistic director for a children's theater in Greenville, South Carolina, along with serving as an adjunct professor in Wofford's theater department. I was, as everybody knew, the baseball player. But it didn't take me long to realize that baseball and the arts both required a ton of commitment, mental and physical strength, and a tremendous amount of discipline. I discovered that I could thrive in both worlds. I didn't know it then, but it was a prelude to what we ask of our Bananas players. *Play hard. Be yourself. Fans First. Entertain Always.*

That was my mindset when I went into that Theater for Youth course at Wofford. The class's awesome teacher, Kerry Ferguson, and I developed an amazing relationship. She gave me roles that were the opposite of being a jock, like the nerdy receptionist. She constantly challenged me and pushed me out of my comfort zone. And it helped me become who I am. No wonder I still like her so much. That's exactly what we do with the Bananas.

One time, I had a tremendous amount of trouble learning my lines for a performance.

"Jesse, I want you to meet me at the theater tomorrow at six o'clock," Kerry told me. "Oh, and one more thing. Bring your baseball glove."

I was like, *What?*

That was Kerry's genius. She told me later that many of her students struggled learning their lines, especially the theater newcomers. So she often suggested saying the lines out loud while doing a mindless, repetitive physical action. It could be jumping rope, cutting vegetables, pulling weeds . . . anything that gets the words off the page, out of the brain, and into the mouth and body. It took away the stress of memorization.

My action was playing catch—something I had done thousands and thousands of times in my life, an easy, mindless task.

Acting, like baseball, is as much mental as it is physical. When Kerry began as an actor, her professor suggested the same thing—connecting the action to the memorization.

Kerry brought her glove, too. She had been a high school soft-ball player. She didn't see many students with the baseball/performance overlap, so she took a little chance. It worked! We played catch for forty-five minutes. I was completely at ease. And I learned the lines. Finally, I was confident.

I felt like I fit in pretty quickly, and Kerry was a big part of that. She believed all of her students could cultivate their cre-ative side, even somebody who was new to the theater scene. Hey, I feel the same way now about prospective Bananas ball-players, not all of whom are natural hams.

Here's how Kerry explained her philosophy:

"While I'm sure Jesse was scared, I don't think he was shy for too long! He didn't need my coaching to feel comfortable. For all my students, I promise that our classroom or rehearsal halls are safe and supportive spaces for everyone. We want to collaborate. Students can try and fail and try again and fail again . . . and keep growing while having fun. I think Jesse felt encouraged and quickly understood he was welcome."

We all hit our stride when we put on an original children's production called *Go to Bed, Amelia Red*. It was some of the best fun I've had in my life.

We wrote and scripted the entire play, built the set, designed the costumes—the whole deal. Our group had gone to see a chil-dren's play in Greenville, South Carolina, and that gave us a feel for it. We all worked together on ideas from scratch, narrowing things down, then focusing on what we really wanted to do.

I put my heart and soul into the project. We rehearsed every night and worked like crazy.

The play was about this little girl, Amelia Red, who was scared to go to sleep because she thought there was a monster under her bed. I portrayed her dog, Rover Red. I was one of two characters that was onstage for the entire play, which was a complete challenge.

I think about these moments when we're asking our Bananas players to step out of their comfort zone and dance on the field. This is not something a traditional baseball player has ever considered—I mean, they grow up in a game of very strict rules and, usually, expectations. I can honestly say I know that feeling. I never saw myself playing a giant, high-energy dog who wore a costume made up of bright blue mopheads. Or, for that matter, a yellow tux. But more on that later.

It was a touching, nice, fun play. Amelia wouldn't go to bed and the show was about all the characters (including the dog) who came into the room to reassure her. There was a twist ending. As it turned out, there *was* a monster under Amelia's bed. But the monster was just as scared of Amelia, and it didn't want to come out. The end of the play was Amelia making friends with the monster, sending a message to the kids that sometimes they imagine things to be very scary, when, in fact, they turn out OK. Sometimes the things that make kids scared are actually exciting and interesting and are things they should engage with.

After the adults in the audience laughed like crazy all night, the ending had them all choked up.

The six shows sold out, which was really cool. Honestly, I had never been more nervous than I was opening night. Though I had played in front of bigger crowds in baseball games, I was out of my mind with nervous energy. At the same time, it was definitely an amazing moment.

"When you do something over and over, you can take the moment for granted," Matt said as he described our play's aftermath. "I remember after opening night, Jesse was just over the moon with energy and excitement. It was like how an athlete must feel after a big game. Jesse was just bouncing off the walls, even more so than normal. This was an accomplishment he wasn't used to. I won't forget that. He put such life and vigor into his role as that big, gregarious, silly dog."

I might have been a fluffy dog, but I took my role very seriously. To play my part well, I had to work on my physical and facial characteristics. I never left the stage. I was the loyal, close (and often terrified) companion of Amelia Red.

My dad called it one of the best weekends of his life. He got to see his son play in a weekend baseball series—like normal—but also appear in two performances of *Go to Bed, Amelia Red.* Baseball and theater? It sounded like an unusual combination, but there were similarities.

The theater ensemble is like a team. Thespians/actors/people/team members collaborate in pairs or as a larger group. Participants learn to work together for a goal and cooperate with others. It's more detailed than it looks. Their timing has to be precise.

Kerry gave me a chance and took me seriously. That gave me confidence, and I learned about how powerful a really good theatrical performance could be, especially for children. There's an obvious parallel with what I'm doing now with the Bananas. In both places, I've never apologized for being myself, even when that has manifested itself in big and bold ways.

"We'd be having a discussion and Kerry would tell Jesse to come back tomorrow with five ideas . . . and he'd come back with seventy-three," Matt said, still laughing about it all these years later.

Kerry has come to several Bananas games over the years, and I know she gets a big kick out of them. She loves how we've been able to mesh the passions for entertainment and baseball.

"It might not seem like such a novel idea now, but intertwining his passions makes sense," Kerry said. "Did I envision the

Savannah Bananas or Banana Ball when Jesse was at Wofford? Of course not. But looking back, I'm not surprised. It has translated perfectly."

Here's what translated perfectly: When we built sets, designed costumes, and worked on the staging—I guess the so-called non-glamorous stuff—I appreciated the totality of a production. All the planning and logistics really matter. They're the difference between an event that is seamless and one that isn't quite there.

Within the Bananas organization, there are many unheralded people who work with merchandise or help fans in the box office or serve the food and beverages or put together our amazing social media presence. The players get noticed—and I certainly do—but our entire team deserves credit for making it all work.

I learned so many valuable lessons at Wofford that help me now with the Bananas. I can talk to all the players as a guy who knows what it takes to compete in a Division I baseball program. But I can also say with authority, "Hey, we're going to do this dance. We're going to do this performance."

I know what it's going to look like and I understand the staging, the blocking, how to be on a microphone. All the terms like *stage left*, I learned that in theater.

It's one of the reasons I work so well with Zack Frongillo, our director of entertainment. He has a background in dance and ballet. He can also play baseball. It's rare, that combination of skills and interests. I was looking for baseball players, obviously, but I was also looking for performers.

With our college team in Savannah—the precursor to the Banana Ball touring team—we did "Dancing with the Future Stars," which was a hit. Our players performed classic or ballroom dancing on the field with a ballet instructor. Some of our guys were a bit leery, but once they got going, they loved it. Like Kerry Ferguson said, everybody can cultivate their creative side.

We also did "Dancing with the Future Stars" when I was general manager of the Gastonia Grizzlies. If I hadn't had the theater background and stage experience, maybe such a thing never would have occurred to me.

Some people have asked, "If you didn't pursue a career in baseball, would you have pursued acting?" I'm not sure I see that necessarily. Whatever people think I have—whether it's creative problem-solving, enthusiasm, fearlessness, patience, imagination, relentlessness, or any other quality—I think it probably came from how I was hardwired. But I needed these very different outlets to find out who I really was.

Theater was great. But baseball was my life. Toward the end of my college career, when the theater was going strong, the baseball began to unravel. It was not how my athletic story was supposed to end. And I would need everything I'd learned onstage, and on the diamond, to get through it all.

Chapter Five

Bored by Baseball

orn labrum.
Man, those were sobering words. My dream was to finish pitching at Wofford College, then get an opportunity to play professional baseball. And in a matter of a few days, I learned that was not going to happen. I had dreamed of getting drafted. Now I didn't know what was ahead for my life.

Googling the term *torn labrum* yields articles that call it "baseball's most fearsome injury" or "a pitcher's death sentence." Everyone knows about Tommy John surgery, but the torn labrum has become a much more debilitating injury.

The labrum is cartilage in the shoulder that cushions the top arm bone. A person with a torn labrum can't throw. It's that simple. When the rotator cuff is also injured, things are worse. And that was my situation.

It was a really tough time. I had an operation with the world-renowned orthopedic surgeon Dr. James Andrews, down in Alabama. I think he has done procedures on every great pitcher in the modern era, along with world-class athletes such as Michael Jordan, Charles Barkley, Emmitt Smith, Allen Iverson,

Jack Nicklaus, Drew Brees, Bo Jackson, and Brett Favre. Frank Jobe invented the Tommy John surgery, but James Andrews really pioneered it. The surgery takes a healthy tendon from an arm or leg to replace the pitching arm's torn ligament. He has done 2,500 Tommy John surgeries on pitchers, but it began when Frank Jobe performed the first one . . . on Tommy John.

I thought my labrum could be fixed, and I visualized a return to the mound, but my injury was just too severe. I was done.

I'm not one of those guys who wants to throw a pity party, but I was seriously bummed. After all the years playing in the backyard with my dad, doing all those drills, improving my skills at the South Shore Baseball Club, traveling with the AAU team, playing high school baseball, getting some looks from professional scouts, then earning a scholarship to Wofford, it was over.

Now what?

I was determined to have a career in baseball, so I thought my next step was getting into coaching. As I got older, I had worked as a hitting and pitching instructor. I did some clinics, and I think the kids liked me. Maybe that was my future.

Then I got this incredible opportunity to coach in the Cape Cod Baseball League, when my college coach made a call on my behalf. The Cape League has always been known as the best college baseball summer league in America. Players from different colleges go to the Cape and play daily games, which are viewed by scouts. Straight out of college, I was named as one of five coaches with the Cotuit Kettleers, a club that produced well-known major-leaguers such as Will Clark, Ron Darling, John Franco, Joe Girardi, Mike Matheny, Jeff Reardon, Tim Salmon, Terry Steinbach, Chase Utley, Greg Vaughn, and Mike Yastrzemski.

I worked for Mike Roberts, a legendary head coach, on a team filled with players destined for the major leagues. I was the fifth assistant coach, a volunteer guy, but I had the best seat in the house. My whole career was in front of me. Who knew where this could lead?

Coach Roberts said he looked for specific qualities in his young assistants—love of the game, enthusiasm, an off-the-charts work ethic, and the knowledge that baseball was a twenty-four-hour-a-day job. He felt I checked all those boxes.

There was just one thing wrong. When we got to the second game of our season, I quickly realized I had a problem with baseball.

I was bored watching baseball. Bored out of my mind.

I hated it.

I knew the game's intricacies. I knew what was going on. I understood what it took to be a good team, and I could communicate with players. But the game was so slow to watch—painfully slow.

I vividly remembered playing the game. When a player is on the mound, that player is in control. A player is a part of the action. You're playing a game.

But sitting in the dugout, watching the game on the field and maybe making a few suggestions, I was bored. And I realized I knew more about what was going on in the game than 99 percent of the fans. I just thought to myself, *Wow, if I grew up loving this game and I'm bored stiff, I can't imagine how everyone else in the stands is feeling. How many people didn't even bother to come to the game because they knew they'd be bored?*

That was my aha moment. To pinpoint exactly when Banana Ball had its origins, rewind to the twenty-three-year-old me and my sudden disillusionment with the game. At that time, I couldn't have imagined anything such as Banana Ball. But for the first time in my life, I saw baseball in a different light. The game had problems. I was already starting to think about the way things could change.

It wasn't something I verbalized much to Mike, who became the super-respected, longtime head coach at the University of North Carolina.

Here's what Mike remembered: "I do not remember him talking about seeing the game in a different light, but we all certainly knew Jesse was a guy with big ideas who wasn't afraid to think outside the box. Is baseball slow? Is it boring? At times, yes. Does it need some adjustments? Absolutely.

"You can say what you will about Jesse, but you can't deny his passion and his willingness to try things. I may or may not agree with some of them, but he has absolute passion, and he loves the game and wants it to thrive. I do know that. A lot of us would like to be known as visionaries, but Jesse is truly a visionary in this game. I can't say I saw something like the Savannah Bananas brewing back then. Who would've imagined that? But Jesse's ambitions and the potential for him to do something big? Oh yeah, we all saw that."

Changing a game that has been around for a century—especially for lifetime baseball people—can be a very difficult thing. I just started seeing a lot of things differently and felt like there was a better way.

All of a sudden, for example, it stunned me to think baseball had a play called a walk. There could be five or six straight pitches—with the hitter not even lifting the bat off his shoulder—and he would then *walk* to first base. The whole process might take several minutes. How did the fans stay awake?

The batter stepped out of the box—after every pitch!—to stretch, adjust his batting gloves, take a practice swing, whatever.

The pitcher took his sweet time. If a runner got on first

base, he might throw over—repeatedly—and fans would boo at the monotony. Meanwhile, some of the things that fans actually loved—the bat flips, the showmanship, the flair—were discouraged.

There had to be a way to make baseball fun, fast, and exciting—not long, slow, and boring. I fell in love with trying to solve that problem. Since early in our ownership of the Bananas, we've had a simple sentence on our website.

We make baseball fun.

That's our mantra and our North Star, along with *Fans First. Entertain Always.*

Our plans have continued to morph through the years. As we got deeper into it, we have discovered new iterations and different possibilities. But it started when I realized I felt sheer boredom when I watched baseball games.

That boredom led me to wonder, *What if there was a game where, you know, everyone could enjoy it? And it wasn't just for the baseball purists and baseball traditionalists. And it wasn't just a place to go in summer.* My thought process led me to realize that our game wasn't just a sports business. We were really in the entertainment business, too.

So I wasn't becoming a coach, after all.

I was still interested in helping the game and developing players, but I found out quickly that the thing I loved most was making an impact, not just mindlessly cashing a paycheck or going through the motions. At the Cape Cod Baseball League, part of my job was working on the field every day. Look, I'm terrible at that stuff. They gave me a riding lawn mower, which was scary, and they told me I'd get paid a little bit of money if I mowed the field. There was no way I wanted to do just that. I wanted to make a bigger impact.

Before I arrived at the Cape, I had gotten an email from the Wofford College athletic department. The minor-league baseball team in Spartanburg was looking for interns. And I was like, *Well, I'm hurt. I can't play anymore. I've committed to coach in the Cape Cod league. But let me look into this.*

It was an unpaid internship. Interns would get a commission if they sold sponsorships, but the team was colossally failing. It was literally on the way out. It was going to play one more year in Spartanburg and then start a new team in Forest City.

I saw the opportunity as a good way to get started. I was looking for a way to impact the game from the top, so the front office became my route. I had all sorts of ideas percolating inside my head. I knew baseball had to create special moments. Nothing matters more than making people feel like they matter. That meant fans, and players; it could be your staff in any business.

From the beginning, I believed in challenging all the boring stuff that usually happens in an office. Like invoices. Can invoices be fun? Everyone has the same invoices, the same terms and conditions and contracts.

It took me a while to make it happen, but we wrote new invoices for the Bananas and now they are definitely on brand.

They read: *Today is your day. There's nothing quite like Bananas payday. You may think you've had days like this, maybe when you bought your first house, maybe when you bought your first car, maybe when you bought your first all-inclusive vacation. So pull out your Bitcoin, check, credit card or rare coins and make that payment like we know you can. This is your moment. Now seize it. Love, Jesse Cole* [or whoever writes the invoice].

Why does it have to be an ordinary invoice?

Why does a voice mail have to be so bland? Why not use different music or try a little fun? You'll start hearing back from your customers, "Hey, that was awesome. I like that." You can't have fun unless you take some chances by doing fun things. Try a new voice mail, a new email signature, new on-hold music, anything. It might give your people and the people they encounter more purpose and more enjoyment connecting with you, your team, and your mission.

But when I walked in the door at Spartanburg, they just wanted me to drum up any revenue I could for the team.

One day, they dropped a telephone book on my desk.

"What's this?" I said.

"These are your potential clients," they told me. "Start calling."

You probably already realize I don't do things halfway.

So I called what felt like every business in the phone book.

Before long, my calendar filled up with meetings. I met with some business owners at their house, and they insisted I meet their pig. I can't remember what they did at that home business and I forget the guy's name, but there was definitely a pig outside in the front yard, just walking around. I remember going to a security company where I convinced them to do the "security save of the game" for $350. I just kept selling and selling and selling.

Looking back, I think I came to grips with the end of my baseball career pretty quickly because I kept busy and stayed motivated. I cared about giving my all to my work, even if it wasn't exactly what people in that role usually did. I was really enthused and driven. It took my mind off my torn rotator cuff. In some ways, maybe the injury became a blessing in disguise.

I made such an impression in Spartanburg that they offered the intern—me—the choice of much bigger jobs. I could become assistant general manager of Forest City, North Carolina, the brand-new team in a brand-new stadium, or general manager of the team in Gastonia, North Carolina. Gastonia was struggling and failing, near the bottom in league attendance.

I chose Gastonia, which was drawing about two hundred fans a game and had $268 in its bank account on my first day.

Why not take the new team and its sparkling stadium, and learn the ropes from the GM, and do it all "right"? Because I knew Gastonia was where I could make the biggest impact. Ken Silver, the owner and still one of my biggest mentors, made me a general manager at twenty-three years old. The assistant GM, Jamie Curtis, had been an intern for Ken the past summer. He knew her really well. Me? Not so much. So I was on a mission to always prove I belonged and that I could help us accomplish special things.

I learned a lot those first few years about finding your passion. At Gastonia, I did everything—operations, food and beverage, hiring, finances—you name it. I came home exhausted at the end of the day.

Probably, I was doing too much. I'd try to put up a tiny little sign, which took me thirty minutes when it would've taken someone else about a minute. I was so bad at that. I was doing things that weren't energizing me—they were depleting me.

It took me several years to learn that if I wanted to have energy in my work, I needed to do things that energized me. These days, I challenge our staff members to do an energy audit on their calendar. What are the things you just don't want to do? Could they be eliminated? Could they be delegated?

I keep a personal energy list. I divide the list into three buckets. One is *creating*, which is coming up with new ideas and promotions. Another is *sharing*, which is doing an interview, giving a keynote speech, or doing a podcast. The third is *growing*, which is listening to podcasts, reading a book, learning something from an outside industry.

If I do all of those three on a given day, look out!

Ken knew that empowering me would also energize me, so he did. At Gastonia, we created a Midnight Madness game. We had a Flatulence Fun Night (we ordered whoopee cushions and had a bean-burrito-eating contest on the field; childish, yes, but very funny). A Salute to Underwear Night (if you wore underwear outside of your pants, you got a prize). We were a lot more than just baseball. We started selling out games. I mean, there were games where no tickets were available, which was wild.

The first game my dad saw at Gastonia, his general manager son was sitting on a platform, daring fans to knock him into the dunk tank. It was all great fun.

Before my first season in Gastonia, the biggest night they had ever had was about eight hundred fans. Our first night, we had eleven hundred fans in the stadium. For that opening night, I strategically did interviews with *every section* of the newspaper. I talked to the editor, the community section, the sports section, and the business section. So the Gastonia Grizzlies were all over that newspaper, and it didn't cost us a dime. I had to maximize things on a tight budget. But maybe that also was a foreshadowing of where we would be media-wise.

Opening night was big. We had a few more big nights. And each year, our efforts grew bigger and bigger, until 2013, when we were fourth in the country in college-summer-league attendance. We averaged between twenty-three hundred and twenty-four hundred fans a game in an old ballpark, which was a really good accomplishment; many sports these days look to open sparkling new stadiums, and fans were coming to us for us, not for where we played.

The success we enjoyed just fueled my passion for finding a

better way to present baseball. I think back to the way I felt about the game when I was young, following the Boston Red Sox with my dad. I was romantic about this game. It was everything to me. When I look at people these days, the kids and the families, I think baseball is losing some appeal. Our world is getting faster and faster. Attention spans are getting shorter and shorter. Major League Baseball is getting longer and slower.

But when I think about how baseball fans view their game, it's like a love story. That's what everything I do has been built on. I know that love has faded for some fans and players, just as it had for myself. And I know how the things we did at Gastonia for ten years helped fans rekindle some of that love. In many ways we were like a warm-up act for what we're still doing with the Savannah Bananas. It's the same motivation, and it comes from the same place. We're trying to explore what the game could be again, while having as much fun as we can along the way.

Here's how Coach Mike Roberts, my former Cape Cod Baseball League boss, put it: "There are people who are dreamers and there are people who are doers. Jesse has constant dreams, but he knows how to put them into action. He shook up Gastonia. He found a community in Savannah that was hungry for something different and now he's going to take this thing all over the nation, if not the world. It's a phenomenon.

"There used to be a guy named Bill Veeck, who tried every innovation under the sun for baseball. He was the guy who had the Chicago White Sox playing in shorts. Some people thought he was crazy, but he was always trying to find a new way to make the game fun for the fans. Jesse Cole is the second coming of Bill Veeck. I'll take it further: I think Jesse is the Steve Jobs of baseball. He just sees the world differently. We need people like that. Baseball needs people like that."

We sure saw things differently in Gastonia, and lots of people picked up on that. In the minor-league baseball industry, there are conferences and gatherings where people share ideas and information. To some degree, everyone has the same obstacles, so it's a good way to see what works well in other markets. I was more than happy to help where I could.

There was one particularly persistent young woman who worked for another minor-league team. She seemed fascinated with the crazy stuff we were trying in Gastonia. She wanted to know more. For a couple of years, we had a pretty regular email conversation.

Her name was Emily McDonald.

She seemed nice. Clearly, she was interested in being successful. I tried to be helpful.

I had no way of knowing what baseball had in store for us.

Chapter Six

Meeting Emily

It seemed like another normal day for Emily McDonald—a young, ambitious, problem-solving, driven, creative, enthusiastic lover of baseball. As usual, she was filled with ideas, some of them crazy. She worked for the Augusta GreenJackets in Georgia. But this day would change her life. (Mine, too.)

Her boss called and got right to the point: "I just met the guy you're going to marry!"

I'm endlessly amazed by fate and how it often brings together two people who are so right for each other. I think they call it "serendipity."

How did Emily and I get together? It's not a short story. It's definitely a good story.

The success in Gastonia was noticed around the minor-league-baseball industry. Everyone was always studying other teams: what's working, what's falling flat. Because of our accomplishments, in 2008, I was speaking at a conference in Charlotte to describe our most popular promotions, like the Grandma Beauty Pageant.

An executive from the Augusta team was in the audience, and

she was taken by our imaginative ideas. I must have made a good impression, too.

Immediately, Emily's boss delivered a scouting report to her: this guy is passionate, all about community, and willing to test new ideas. Emily had the same values. In fact, she sounded like my female alter ego. And, of course, we both worked in minor-league baseball.

Emily's boss was insistent. "I just met the guy you're going to marry. You're going to either marry him or bounce ideas off him. Come on, just email him."

So Emily did.

I remember reading her first email: "Hi, this is Emily McDonald with the Augusta GreenJackets. My boss sent me this video of you speaking at the Summer Ball Classic. She told me about your Grandma Beauty Pageant. We're always trying to work with seniors. I'd love to hear how you did it and how you got people excited about it."

That was it. The kind of typical business communication that somebody might read. It *might* trigger a response. Or they might just get busy with other things and forget about it altogether.

I loved the fraternal relationships in minor-league baseball, the shared ideas, the way people tried to help because, really, we were in the same business.

So I replied to Emily, trying to help the best I could. Back and forth we went. A complete email relationship. We were all business, focused on the entertainment aspect of baseball, an exchange of ideas, some thoughts about things to try.

It could've stopped there.

But in 2010, Emily contacted me to say she was coming up for a Charlotte Knights game. We were not far away in Gastonia, so she wanted to drop by, check out our stadium, and introduce herself. Sure, I said. I told her I would love to meet her in person.

The next thing I knew, it was June 10, 2010, a blazing-hot day. Emily showed up. And as she looked down on the field, she saw me for the first time. I was teaching the "Thriller" dance to our Grizzlies players as part of our Salute to Michael Jackson Night.

Here's how Emily remembers it: "There was no one around, so I came to the field. I saw what was going on, and I was like, *What is happening? Who is this guy?*"

It was probably one hundred degrees that day, and I was dripping with sweat. I introduced myself and was glad to see her. She loved minor-league baseball, just like me. I thought she was quite attractive, and she had a lot of energy, just like I imagined from our email exchanges. She seemed like a lot of fun.

We were both in relationships, and neither of us was looking at the other as a romantic partner, but we'd been corresponding about promotions, and I looked forward to talking with her about the industry later that evening, after I was done working at the game. As it turned out, though, she didn't even stay for our game. After I gave her a tour of our ballpark, she left to go to the Charlotte Knights game.

So, back to email. Flash forward to 2011, to the Minor League Baseball promotional seminar in Myrtle Beach, South Carolina. When I walked through the door, I spotted her immediately. Emily, too, looked across the room, and our eyes met. The only thing missing was the musical soundtrack. Emily later described it like a scene from a movie.

"Emily?" I whispered, but I'm not sure any sound came out of my mouth.

When I walked in, Emily was the only woman in sight— literally. She was sitting at a table full of guys and was wearing a hoodie and a baseball cap. She was basically running the table, and everybody wanted to talk to her.

I hadn't seen Emily in more than a year. That night, we both went to dinner with a big group of people, and the group started shrinking as the night progressed. There were just a few people when we headed over to the stadium, and by the time we wound up back at a dueling-pianos bar, it was just Emily and me.

At that point, it was game over for me.

We spent the whole weekend talking about ideas and sitting together in the seminar sessions, just brainstorming. We both had such passion for the game and how to promote it. The mutual admiration started there. The mutual attraction started there. We were so in awe of what the other one was trying to do.

Emily came from a one-stoplight, no-fast-food town in western New York called Marathon, which is about forty miles out of Syracuse. She had a sports-minded family with three brothers, and it wasn't surprising that she had learned early how to play ball. Emily and each of her brothers had been part of state championship teams in high school. She was naturally drawn to sports and had already been thinking about a sports-related career when she left for SUNY Oneonta to major in marketing, public relations, and communications.

Right out of college, she landed a marketing position for a technology firm in Binghamton, New York. With a really good salary and a big title on her impressive-looking business card, she was off and running, right? Yeah, not really. Emily was miserable.

She was stuck in a cubicle. She stared at a screen all day, every day. Her job was very corporate, very serious. Her coworkers were older and very techie-oriented. She had thought it would be different when she was hired, but it was not her vibe at all.

Emily discovered her passion at the local Binghamton team,

the Double A affiliate of the New York Mets. She picked up a
night job working at the Binghamton games, selling tickets, food,
promotions, anything. From 4:00 p.m. to 11:00 p.m., she loved
her life. The problem was the day job, the 8:00 a.m. to 4:00 p.m.
She hated the routine. Even then, she instinctively knew corporate life was not for her. So Emily showed courage and she quit.
She followed her passion and was hired full-time with Ripken
Baseball, an organization founded by Cal Ripken Jr. that owned
three minor-league teams and also staged tournaments and
events, developing young baseball players. Initially, she did ticket
sales, a natural entry point, at Ripken headquarters in Aberdeen,
Maryland.

The organization's leadership realized pretty quickly that Emily was good, so they offered her a position at her choice of three
sites. She could go to their Florida location, the site of spring
training. She could stay at Aberdeen, which was the organization's bread and butter. They also had a spot in Augusta, which
was really struggling and needed help.

Emily chose Augusta because she wanted to fix something
and build it up. She didn't want a shiny new place, like in Florida
or Aberdeen.

Well, her career path got my attention. I had made the *same*
decision when I took over the hopelessly struggling Gastonia club
instead of choosing the safer route and becoming second-in-
command at a brand-new ballpark. We both saw value in building and innovating and not just maintaining.

When Emily told me about her path in baseball, it all made
sense.

Things weren't always perfect. She was occasionally frustrated with affiliated baseball, especially when her good ideas
were ignored. If things didn't originate or hadn't been approved at

the major-league level, well-meaning administrators couldn't do the things they wanted to serve their specific market. I think this is why we empower our Bananas staff so much now. We don't believe in red tape or bureaucracy. If one of our staff members has a good idea, they don't need a sounding board or a committee. They are instructed to go for it. Why not?

Emily and I saw eye to eye on so many things. So when our paths finally had intersected, there was no turning back. Shortly after our meetup in Myrtle Beach, we ended our other relationships. From that moment forward, we talked every day.

We were officially dating, but we kept it a secret.

I told my dad I had met someone special, and we all had dinner together the next time he came to North Carolina.

My dad said he remembers everything being great. He and his wife "loved Emily from day one," but they were puzzled why we couldn't be more open with the relationship.

"We're at dinner, and Jesse and Emily are looking over their shoulders to see if anyone's around that knows them," my dad said. "I mean, we thought Jesse had hit the lottery. Emily's personality and ability to make everyone feel at ease and comfortable was just wonderful. The whole thing about going incognito with their relationship, I didn't get that. But I guess they had their reasons."

We did have our reasons. I thought we were destined to work together all along, but Emily fought that. She fought it hard. She wasn't interested in coming in and just being someone's girlfriend. She was making a name for herself in baseball. She didn't want to be handed anything.

We talked about it for a long time. She had been working for a team in Vermont, and we kept discussing the topic. Should she quit there and move to Charlotte? Should she work for Gastonia and just not tell anybody? She considered starting over in a different industry and helping teams as a part-time worker or volunteer.

I never thought that was a realistic option. In the back of her mind, Emily knew she was destined to work in Gastonia. She just had to get comfortable with the idea. She didn't want to act impulsively. Emily's decision process took several months.

I finally told her, "Come on, I know you want to work here. We can do something special together."

We talked about it one night, and I was going for the commitment. I asked Emily, "What would be your dream job? What could you do for our team?"

She thought about it and said, "I don't know. I think I just want to help people have fun. It's fun to create fun."

So I immediately chimed in: "Great! We need a Director of Fun!"

That's where the title was born. In 2011, Emily became Gastonia's Director of Fun. She was on board. We took pictures of her in a hot dog costume. That was her business card. She did community relations, ticket sales, and anything else that was needed.

Meanwhile, it became increasingly hard to keep our relationship a secret, but it was important to both of us that Emily got the proper respect and wasn't just viewed as "Jesse's girlfriend." We kept it a secret for more than a year.

My roommate knew, and her roommate knew. After six to nine months, people started to suspect or ask a lot of questions. We were very professional at all times. But most people could just tell something was up by the way we laughed together, had fun together, and spent time together.

About a year after our relationship began, I told Emily that I loved her. It was during a trip to Charleston, South Carolina, and weirdly, we were standing outside a bathroom, which wasn't a really nice setting. We still laugh about the timing. I wish I could say we were walking down the beach at sunset. Hey, love is love.

When we first met, we talked about all our dreams for the industry. As we progressed, we were involved with numerous teams and we remained aligned. We'd go to concerts or on trips, but there was no diversion from our passion. We still talked about baseball dreams.

Obviously, the dreams have reached a higher level with the creation of the Bananas. But from the beginning, we were so in love with what we could do in the industry. I had never seen that passion from another woman.

At first, we thought the dream was having numerous teams, but then we realized that was not for us. We preferred to concentrate on one team. We worked with some teams that were difficult and consuming. They really beat us up. We called those "learning experiences."

We had a vision of baseball bringing families together, bringing team members together, and hopefully bringing together families all over the world. We didn't know it back then, but we were on a path to do just that, with the Savannah Bananas.

As I got to know Emily, I was amazed at how perfectly we complemented each other. We had a strong yin and yang. I'm an only child. She has a bigger family with three younger brothers. I've got a big personality, and I'm always promoting something. She's the one who likes to help people and take care of them.

We had great years together in Gastonia. We grew and developed an appreciation for our differences and quirks. When she saw me going more to her preferences and not being so impulsive, she had a bigger love and admiration for me. When she understood my perspective and awareness, my love for her grew. We learned how to manage our differing personalities.

All of these factors made it so obvious: Emily was going to be my wife. I was going to propose. But, being me, the proposal wouldn't be an ordinary operation in any way.

It had to be over-the-top.

I knew I wanted it to happen during our last game of the season in 2014.

My first issue was buying the ring. Emily didn't wear jewelry— at all. Good luck trying to figure out what kind of ring to get for a girl who doesn't wear jewelry, doesn't care about jewelry, and doesn't want jewelry. All of her family and friends knew she placed her highest value in nonmaterial things. I had no idea what to do.

I started bringing up people we knew who were getting married. When I heard about an engagement, I would say to Emily, "Did you see that ring?" I started saying things I would never say, like, "Did you like that it had all those diamonds around it?"

And she would say, "Oh, no, I would never want to have anything like that."

So slowly but surely, I gathered some hints on what she liked (and many more on what she didn't). When I felt secure enough, I got the ring.

My next step was to involve both our entire families as well as all of our closest friends. I thought it would be pretty easy for everyone to show up at the last game of the year because it wouldn't look too suspicious to Emily. I could sell the fact to Emily that our family and friends were coming to celebrate the end of another great season.

As a last-game tradition, we always brought the whole staff on the field to recognize them individually. I planned to save Emily's introduction for last, and at that point, I would present her with the ring. I arranged to have a baseball cut in half and hollowed out to resemble a ring case. I planned to give her the baseball to open—there would be the ring.

Of course, I wanted to have a fireworks show. No celebration is complete without fireworks. The problem: Emily did all our permits for the fireworks, so I had to go completely behind her back to get approval from the fire department.

It took a lot of extra work and planning, just so Emily wouldn't catch on. Every day, I found myself imagining what the big day would be like. I tried to think of what could go wrong or if it would rain. I wondered if we could pull it off, and I didn't want it to be typical or average. I wanted it to stand out—for it to be a moment she'd remember forever.

Chapter Seven

Marrying Emily

The proposal was set for August 4, 2014.

The families, friends, and I had done a good job of keeping Emily off the scent of my proposal surprise, which was no small feat. We had both families coming—along with lots of close friends—but she didn't suspect a thing.

We almost had a clean getaway until the night of the proposal. The proposal plan was in full swing by game time. I planned to ask her during the seventh-inning stretch, but Gastonia took a 9–0 lead in the first inning. When our half of the first took more than forty-five minutes, I wasn't sure the game would *ever* end.

By nine o'clock, the game had reached only the fifth inning, and fans were already leaving. Some of our friends even asked, "Can we go home now?" I told them not yet but couldn't stand the wait myself, so we moved the proposal up to the sixth inning. We got everybody mobilized to set up the on-field recognitions in the sixth. Where was Emily? She was popping popcorn. So I hustled back there and had to work to get her attention.

"Emily, we had to move up the on-field stuff. We need you down on the field," I told her.

Typical Emily. She practically rolled her eyes at me. Without missing a beat, she said, "No, I've got stuff to do here. I don't need any recognition."

We were actually fighting over it because she didn't want to leave the fans who wanted their popcorn. She got a little perturbed and said, "OK, fine. But I'm coming right back here after you do your thing."

One by one, I introduced the staff members quickly, saving Emily for last. Then, it hit me: This was the field where we had met in person for the first time, when I was teaching the "Thriller" dance to our players just four years ago. This was the field where we worked together and shared the dreams of what we wanted next.

I said, "Last but not least, I want to recognize our Director of Fun, Emily McDonald. Not many of you know this, but we met right here on this field. I've had the time of my life with you."

I dropped to one knee.

"Emily, in front of my family, your family, and our entire baseball family, will you make me the luckiest guy in the world? Will you do me the honor of becoming my wife?"

I think Emily was stunned. She never said yes. She ran over to hug and kiss me; then the fireworks started going off.

Unfortunately, the wind was blowing in and the fireworks came too close to the field. It delayed the game for about twenty minutes. The umpires and players could only watch and wait.

After that epic proposal, what does Emily do? For most women, it would be *their* moment, right? Between the surprise proposal and the end of a season's worth of grind, Emily planned a weekend getaway for us—to Savannah.

Savannah is full of historical sites, beaches, and amazing restaurants, not to mention the twenty-two town squares in the city's beautiful downtown area.

Emily and I went to a ballpark.

We are hopeless ballpark romantics, ballpark nerds, or whatever we would be called. We're intrigued with how things work at different facilities. And we had a great ballpark to check out—historic Grayson Stadium, built in 1926, a place where Babe Ruth, Lou Gehrig, Jackie Robinson, and Hank Aaron once played. I looked at this massive stadium with the giant brick columns and I was just blown away. To me, it might as well have been Fenway Park.

"This is epic," I told Emily. "Look at this place. It's beautiful."

Savannah has had about a dozen different minor-league teams in the last century. None of them ever really worked. When Emily and I were there, the Savannah Sand Gnats, the Class A affiliate of the New York Mets, certainly weren't working. There were maybe a hundred or so fans in the ballpark, along with a complete absence of noise. Even the music sounded depressing.

The whole place seemed tired. The groundskeepers looked tired. The staff looked tired. Even the players looked tired. Tumbleweeds could've been blowing across that field. It just seemed wrong.

We sat underneath the main grandstand above the third-base dugout, just Emily and I, with plenty of room to spread out in the green general admission seats. I was surprised to see how dead it was. No, I was *shocked*. I was like a kid in a candy store because this stadium was larger than life for me. At Gastonia, we were used to a high school field with zero amenities. This was like a baseball palace. But where was everybody?

We looked around and thought, *Wow, what a shame.* Grayson Stadium seemed so majestic, and there was a definite awesome feel to just being there. It was Saturday night, about eighty-two degrees, in a great city, an incredible setting for baseball . . . and no one was there!

"Emily, this place would be amazing for us!" I blurted out.

"We can't come here, Jesse," Emily said, shaking her head. "They already have a team."

I wasn't going to hear it.

"Well, what if this team leaves?" I said. "What then? If the Sand Gnats leave town, that could be our shot. I'm serious."

Emily was in no mood for a debate. "Whatever," she said, and turned her attention back to the field.

Emily knew a team exec, who came over to sit with us for a few innings. The exec complained about everything—the state of Grayson Stadium, the lack of fan support. To top it off, there were zero promotions, and I don't remember seeing a mascot. You could tell that the exec didn't even want to be there. The whole thing was a flat experience.

We could have left the ballpark, continued with our weekend, and not given it a second thought. I wasn't quitting on this idea. I was motivated to send a text to Justin Sellers, commissioner of the Coastal Plain League.

Me: Hey, we're in Savannah at Grayson Stadium. If the Sand Gnats ever leave this town, we're calling it right now. We want this stadium and this market. This is just amazing.
Justin: Sounds good.

We'd heard rumblings that the team was fighting with the city about building a new ballpark. It would've been an approximately $40 million project—no small chunk of change—but the city wasn't budging because the attendance was so poor.

I wasn't even thinking about a new ballpark. Grayson Stadium had such potential. And I thought Savannah was the kind of place where baseball could work—if it were done the right way.

"Imagine what we could do here, Emily," I said.

Emily just smiled and took another sip of her drink. She wanted to see the ballpark and enjoy a game, a casual night out for some celebration. Our lives had changed because I had proposed to her just six days earlier. In my mind, our lives were about to change again.

"It's a really nice ballpark," Emily said, probably trying to humor me. "But let's be realistic here."

"I am being realistic," I said. "I've never seen anything more clearly. This ballpark should be our canvas. This ballpark should be *ours.*"

Savannah is one of America's unique towns. It has food. It has history. It has landmarks throughout its downtown. It's where the Girl Scouts began. One of the benches is where Tom Hanks sat to tell the story of Forrest Gump. Savannah is such a melting pot of creative people when it comes to food and the arts. There's culture, openness, and inclusion. When John Berendt wrote the book *Midnight in the Garden of Good and Evil*, which was later turned into a movie, Savannah's tourism exploded. And it hasn't stopped.

Very rarely do people say anything negative about today's Savannah. It's a party city. The annual Saint Patrick's Day parade, which began in 1824, should be a bucket list event for everyone. Marching bands, dancers, and people riding elaborate floats come to Savannah from all over the world. People wear crazy costumes, bright wigs, and face and body paint. Some years, more than half a million people descend upon the city for one of America's largest Saint Patrick's Day celebrations.

It's an open-bar, open-container town—sort of like New Orleans and Key West—where you can barhop without having to finish your drink in the place where you purchased it. You can eat, drink, celebrate, and just have fun. Few places in America have more bachelorette parties than Savannah.

It was very random for Emily to pick Savannah as our getaway destination. I think it just happened to be convenient and right down the highway for us. But once we had gotten down there to see that ballpark, once we had sampled how special the city really was, it sort of clicked. There was intentionality about my thinking.

Emily finally agreed—or at least she bought into the dream: Savannah was the kind of place where we'd love to have a team. If Savannah ever came open, we would definitely be interested. We let city officials know our thoughts and mentally filed it away; we had a wedding to plan.

And speaking of that, where would we get married?

The ballpark.

Shocker!

That sounds like something the groom would push for, only to be refused. But in our case, the bride was all-in on a ballpark wedding.

Emily and her bridesmaids went on a cruise for the bachelorette party. Me? Vegas, baby! My eleven best men and I hopped a flight to Las Vegas. Yep, that is correct—I had eleven best men. I didn't like the idea of separating the groomsmen and the best man, so I made them all best men.

Around the Vegas Strip, we wore Gastonia Grizzlies tuxedo

uniforms, which we had designed because we wanted to be known as the best-dressed team in sports. I thought it would be cool, but it blew up in our faces. The bouncers saw us coming—twelve dudes in Grizzlies tuxedo uniforms—and said, "You ain't coming into our place." We got rejected by every single club on the Strip. Maybe it would've been different if we had been twelve girls. But we were a bunch of dudes dressed up like idiots. Every bouncer just shook his hand at us and said, "It's not happening, gentlemen." We still had a fun experience.

Emily and I exchanged vows on Saturday, October 10, 2015, at the Gastonia ballpark. The absolute perfect touch was getting married by Ken Silver, owner of the Gastonia Grizzlies, the man who had brought me in as an intern, then hired me as the team's general manager. Ken and Bette Silver are such wonderful people and they have been the biggest confidants and mentors to Emily and me.

Some people were surprised when Ken officiated at the ceremony. They had had no idea he was an ordained minister. Actually, I think he took an online test. Anyway, he was legitimate.

Everything about our wedding day was perfect.

Even the monsoon.

That would normally take the starch out of an outdoor wedding, right? Not for Emily and me. A rainy day at the ballpark somehow seemed appropriate. Some people think a rainy wedding day is actually good luck and a sign of a strong marriage.

Emily and her bridesmaids arrived in a limousine, which almost got stuck in the mud. Other women might have been stressing and thinking the day was a complete disaster. Emily was laughing and enjoying herself the whole time. People kept asking her, "Do you want to put it off? Do you want to move it somewhere else?"

And Emily was like, "No way! This is where we want to have our wedding. This is our life."

We invited close to two hundred people. I believe we had a bit more than that because this was a public ballpark and a few people invited themselves.

For the record, I *did not* wear a yellow tux to our ceremony.

We all had a great time. My dad stood behind Ken Silver, holding an umbrella over us as we said our vows. Bette Silver sang. And it never stopped raining.

The infield completely flooded. The roof of the big tent in center field we had for the reception held up adequately, but there was so much water on the ground that guests' feet wound up soaking wet. Most people kicked off their shoes. After a while, guests embraced the situation and enjoyed the reception. Some of them played in the rain.

For our first dance, Emily and I chose "Love Is an Open Door" from Disney's *Frozen*. It was a duet. Every line meant something to us, especially the ones about us both searching to find our place and how we found that in each other.

After a few beers, some of the guests went running and sliding into the grass right behind shortstop, where there was a pretty good-size puddle. I remember a few nice face-plants right into that small lake.

Our wedding started at five o'clock. We had the DJ until eleven—when the fireworks began, miraculously just after the rain had stopped—and I kept paying him cash to go an extra thirty minutes. After three times, he was out of music. My dad said he'll always cherish how all eleven of the best men gave speeches.

"Some were just incredible, really touching, just beautiful," my dad said. "Some were absolute laugh riots. I loved every one of them.

"You could just sense in that tent the great feelings everyone had for Emily and Jesse. I think everyone knew it was going to be a special couple. The party eventually made it back to the hotel about twelve thirty. I remember being up until about three thirty in the morning, which is really unusual for me, but we all had so much fun laughing and talking with each other. I will always remember how Emily and Jesse began their life together in such a perfect way."

Well, most of it was perfect, anyway.

The week of the wedding was big overall, and we had to compart-mentalize to concentrate on it.

Officials from the city of Savannah refused to budge on the Sand Gnats' demand for a stadium to replace Grayson, and the Sand Gnats' ownership fled town and relocated to Columbia, South Carolina, where that city had agreed to build them a new stadium. That meant the rights to Savannah's market were available. We had been working with city officials since the spring of 2015 on the possibility of moving an expansion franchise to Savannah, and five days before our wedding, we received the keys and took over Grayson Stadium.

We joined the Coastal Plain League and started a summer college team. Guys would come from college teams all over the country and get some exposure that they hoped would get them noticed by professional scouts. We had to pay a substantial entry fee to the league in installments, and it helped that we had an excellent track record in Gastonia, along with three years of help-ing Ken Silver to manage a team in Martinsville, Virginia.

We were beyond excited.

They say that faith is the ability to believe in something before you can see it. Well, we must have been the most faithful group around. Somehow, we got two more believers to join us in our dream. Jared Orton, our team president, was thrilled to help build an organization from the ground up. He had started working with us in Gastonia and believed in our vision enough to take a chance on Savannah. Marie Matzinger was one of the smartest people in her high school and college. Just out of school, she was taking a job with this unproven team and market. I know her parents thought she was crazy. But she was a believer, too. That's all we needed.

Or so we thought.

On October 5, 2015, the day we got the keys to Grayson Sta-dium, we received our first jolt of reality. The city workers handed us a pile of keys and said, "Good luck, guys." You could see their smirks. They had little faith in us.

Jared was holding this huge bundle of keys, and they were barely labeled. It took us a while to figure out which one opened the main gate. Where did we even start? As we walked around, it almost looked like a war zone. We quickly realized that every-thing had been taken out of the stadium. The telephone lines and Internet lines had been cut—literally cut with scissors—and all we had were the little stubs of plastic casing and copper wires coming out of the wall.

All the equipment for the video board was gone (even though the previous team was moving to a new stadium). There were no desks in the offices or anywhere, no chairs, nowhere to sit and work. There were tiles missing. The ceiling was leaking. We had a massive job on our hands.

"Well, I guess we can work with this," Marie said, breaking the silence as the rest of us looked around, shell-shocked.

"You know, maybe a minor point, but we are going to need someplace to sit," Jared said, rubbing his chin in thought.

"Wait, what about that picnic table we saw outside at the park?" Emily said, trying to lighten the mood. "Let's pull it in here. We can sit there—at least for now."

So we walked outside and dragged that picnic table into the office. We kept surveying the scene. There was an abandoned trailer, which was truly disgusting. There were no phones, no Internet, no chairs, no tables, like . . . nothing. The place was really barren. The stands weren't in the best condition, and the field was a mess.

"OK, what do we do now?" Emily said, keeping us on task. "How do we start?"

"Well, we've got our cell phones," Jared said. "We can make our calls."

"But who are we going to call?" Marie said with a heavy sigh.

In the stadium, the seats had stickers with the names of season ticket holders. There were billboards with the names of sponsors. We didn't know if those sponsors actually *paid anything* or maybe they had just been supportive of the team a few years ago. But we got our clipboards and wrote down all the names and telephone numbers. These were our first prospects.

"Look, we have to start somewhere," I said.

Jared was stoic like always, constantly studying the situation. Emily and Marie were probably more alike. Emily always believed we could figure things out. Marie did, too, but she was very practical. Me? I was a lofty, big thinker.

"We've got to make the best of this," I said. "Hey, think of it as this big adventure. We have some things to work with. We do.

We're smart people. We know how to work. It's only going to get better. Not everything here is awful."

There was this huge locker room where some of the greatest players in the game had suited up. There was a room for the washer and dryer. There were showers and an extra training room. There was even a place for a merchandise store. We didn't have anything like that in Gastonia.

We were young and optimistic. We didn't really know how these transitions were supposed to work. Marriage, moving, and job changes are often cited as primary stressors in life; they are the kinds of things that can make people lose their minds. Emily and I went through all of them—marriage, job change, moving— in a week.

That's because we lost our house.

I'm eternally grateful for one idea I had back then. One of the best things I did in the first year of our marriage was writing something each day—all 365—then assembling the entries into a book and presenting it to Emily on our first anniversary.

Each morning before Emily woke up, I woke up early to write something that had happened the previous day. She had no idea I was doing this. From one day to the next, I had no idea what would lie ahead. My idea was to document every day of our journey in the first year. Three months later, we ran out of money. Our account was overdrawn. We had to sell our house. We had to empty our savings account and sleep on an air bed in a god-forsaken studio apartment that was our only housing option because it was all we could afford. We budgeted about $30 to buy food for the entire week. We were tapped out.

I remember the day—I remember the exact time of day—when we got the bad news.

It was January 15, 2016. We were in Belleville, New Jersey, for a wedding. Emily and I had just showered. I was putting on my suit (not yellow). Emily was getting into her dress. Then at four forty-five, the cell phone rang.

It was Alex McDonald, Emily's brother who was watching our accounts with the teams in Savannah and Gastonia because we still had them both. More than anyone, Alex knew exactly what was going on.

"Jesse, we're about to miss payroll, and we're overdrafting the account," Alex said, trying to be as composed and professional as he could be.

"What?" I said. "That can't be."

"There's no money in the account," Alex said.

It was Friday afternoon. I quickly transferred some money from another account so we could do the bare minimum and take care of our people.

Then I looked at Emily and said, "We're about to get on a bus for a wedding. We just found out we're out of money, and we're about to miss payroll. But we can't think any more about this right now. We have to go."

Emily and I started walking, not saying a word, but we were in each other's thoughts. Then all of a sudden, we were greeted by all of my college friends and the party was on. We were on the bus, going to the wedding, and we had to momentarily forget about the shocking news we'd just heard from Alex.

So we smiled and laughed. We were fine. We enjoyed it as best we could. It was a fun wedding, and we got some sleep before the long car ride from New Jersey back to North Carolina. I remember it was a very gray morning, no sun at all, completely overcast. As we drove, there was no talking in the car. None. That's very unusual for Emily and me. We're always sharing our thoughts, making plans, playing music, something, anything. Not this time. It was stone silence.

As we drove over a bridge, after about forty minutes of un-easiness, Emily spoke up.

"Jesse, we have to sell our house."

It took me a few seconds to process that. I let Emily's words sit there for a bit; then I answered back.

"You're right. You're absolutely right."

We needed money to put into our new team. We had to figure this out right now. We shifted into logistics mode: How do we sell the house as soon as possible? How do we put it on the market? How do we explain to our families what we're doing? Where are we going to stay in Savannah?

The whole ride home, we were working out those details. I decided to empty out my retirement account on that Monday, so we could put money in the team's account immediately.

I'm sure there are young married couples who have been through a financial crisis—probably a lot worse than the one we faced—but the amazing thing to me was Emily's complete con-viction and confidence in what needed to be done.

She didn't say, "Jesse, this is ridiculous. We've got to sell our team, so we can save our dream house and have our security."

She said, "Jesse, we have to sell our house."

Emily's whole family lived in Charlotte, so we weren't just selling our house. We were selling Emily's identity. That was her decision. We were moving to Savannah. We were going to make this team work.

We weren't going to let anyone talk us out of it. My dad would have said, "No, don't take money out of your retirement fund. Don't sell your house. You can find another option."

When we got back to Savannah, I pulled Jared aside and told him what we were doing. We stood just outside the third-base dugout, by the gate leading to our stadium club. Jared looked at me like somebody had just kicked his dog. He was so sad.

"I'm so sorry," Jared finally said. I think in some way he felt like he had let me down.

There wasn't time to feel sorry for ourselves. We didn't ask for anybody's advice. We knew what we had to do. We came up with a plan. And we went for it.

There wasn't another option. We had gone into big debt to buy the team, and we owed the league a lot of money. We already had a lease with the city for the stadium. We had people who moved down to Savannah to work with our team. We were a few weeks away from announcing our team name. There was no backing down. We couldn't tiptoe around this. We had to move forward with some pretty decisive action steps.

It was definitely a tense time. When Emily and I look back through the book where I detailed our first year of marriage, it's hard to tell how bleak things really were. My focus was on the future and what it would all mean in ten or twenty years. Everything was so optimistic.

People ask us now, "How did you deal with all the things that went wrong? How did you work together?" We really had no other choice but to do our best and work together as a team. We were married. We had the same goals. I think it's our natural demeanor to look on the bright side and know that there is always hope. The glass was always a little bit more full than empty, even when things seemed very bad.

Tough times can test marriages, no question about it. It's really challenging when couples don't know how to work together. It's so important to establish priorities and keep from crossing over into each other's lanes. Not that we were perfect, but I think we realized how important it was to communicate and respect each other at all times. When couples have challenges with business or money, it's pretty easy to be at each other's throats. We never let it get like that because we had mutual respect and really worked to communicate.

Emily is the realistic person in the relationship. While we both have characteristics of dreamers, Emily is usually the one to rein me in. I might say—very seriously—that I want our Bananas players to skydive to their positions. Then Emily will nod her head and say, "OK, well . . . that's interesting, but it might be a little unrealistic and dangerous, so, um, maybe we should rethink that."

We have taken a lot of personality tests to help with our communication skills. I'm the dreamer. Emily is the refiner. She can take one of my ideas, smooth it out, and make it workable. She's always going to err on the side of practicality. Emily has learned the best way to communicate with me—and it's not by carelessly squashing my dreams. That hurts. She knows how to cushion the fall and bring me along to a compromise.

I have become very good at thanking Emily for all that she does, but I need to do it even more often. We have different responsibilities and different things we're really passionate about. I think I am an eternal optimist. Not that Emily is negative, but I think my ridiculous optimism has rubbed off on her, so she doesn't dwell on things or aim for perfection all the time. I think I've learned how to meet Emily where she is, maybe take a step back at times and understand her perspective. She is the same way with me. That's with the Bananas and in our personal lives.

The most successful married couples say they never stop working on their relationships. You've got to communicate. You've got to talk things out. Try to understand your partner. These qualities are just as important in the good times as they are in the bad times.

Three months into our marriage, Emily and I were in a new city, broke, and nearly eating shoe leather to survive. We had sunk everything into a college summer-league team in Savannah and no one thought we had a chance. Truly, Emily and I felt like all we had was each other. And that was enough.

Plus, there was a way out. Emily and I had a path in mind, something that had never been done before. Inspired by Walt Disney, P. T. Barnum, and Bill Veeck—three of my heroes and legendary men I had never met—we set out together to plan the route.

Stepping back, I realize that we also had the wisest, most understanding mentors—Ken and Bette Silver. They had an amazing ability for saying the right words and leading us in the proper direction to find the answers ourselves. Ken had hired me in Gastonia, when the team had $268 in the bank and we drew about two hundred fans per game. Our entire staff in Gastonia had turned the team into something special.

The same thing was going to happen in Savannah.

Chapter Eight

The Mentors

For three summers, we had operated and managed the Martinsville Mustangs, a Virginia team in the Coastal Plain League. There was a lot of juggling and maneuvering, but it was great experience. In fact, I feel like I was constantly working on my unofficial doctorate in business, marketing, public relations, and common sense. Class was held in the front seat of Ken Silver's Jeep Grand Cherokee. Night after night—sixty of them in all— we drove from Gastonia, North Carolina, to Martinsville, Virginia, and then back, two hours and change each way.

We started on Interstate 85 North, then the I-485 bypass to avoid the Charlotte traffic, north on I-77, cutting over on I-40 East, up on Highway 68 North and onto the stretch of US 220 North straight into Martinsville. We did that so often, I think we saw those NASCAR back-roads signposts in our sleep.

Huntersville . . . Statesville . . . Winston-Salem . . . Greensboro . . . Madison . . . Stoneville . . . Ridgeway

We stopped for gas at least once each trip, usually at a place on the way home, the Sheetz convenience store, where we swung a sponsorship deal to get free food—sandwiches, cheesesteaks, chicken, anything we wanted (and I usually tried everything). One late night, we saw those dreaded police cruiser lights in the rearview mirror and got pulled over for speeding. It's a wonder it didn't happen more often.

It seems like a blur now—all those back-and-forth trips to oversee the minor-league team in Martinsville. Some people might have passed the time listening to the radio or snoozing. Not me. This was the opportunity of a lifetime, me absorbing so many life lessons from Ken, along with just about everything he had learned about running a baseball team.

I was still a punk kid, not long out of college, full of wild ideas and willing to do whatever it took to make my dreams come true. Banana Ball wasn't even a glint in my eye. I needed experience. I needed assurance. Yeah, I knew deep down, a little shot of con-fidence wouldn't hurt, either.

Ken Silver—my boss and my friend—became my greatest in-fluence and an invaluable sounding board. He believed in me and transformed me from an intern to the twenty-three-year-old general manager of the Gastonia Grizzlies.

Ken's magic formula? He listened. Sometimes, I just needed to talk things out, to get either an affirmative nod or the reaction I heard so often: "Well, what do you think is the right decision, Jesse?" Ken did more than give my crazy notions a safe place to land. He taught me to think for myself.

There is the need for good mentors these days. When college graduates enter the workforce, it can comfort them to lean on someone who already has walked their path and can tell them the truth.

Ken and his wife, Bette, are still the best mentors for Emily and me, even though they are deservedly retired now and spend most of their time cruising around the world. But during our time with Ken and Bette, they prepared us to become effective mentors for our people in Savannah. They trusted us so much.

"What do you guys think?" Ken and Bette asked that every time we faced a crossroads. They taught us how to have faith in our people, how to take a step back and how to treat them like family. They've been married for more than fifty years, so we saw their example of a healthy relationship, too.

We stay in touch often through phone calls, text messages, or social media. Every couple of years, we try to hang out with them for a week or so at their time-share in Mexico. They owned eight different minor-league teams during their career—Ken and Bette have completely divested in their retirement—and there's so much someone like me can gain from their advice and mentorship.

Many mentors are like family, always available for advice. Other mentors you never meet at all.

Some days, I get my guidance from ghosts. I really look up to Walt Disney, P. T. Barnum, and Bill Veeck. These were legendary marketers and promoters. They influence me every day.

My office resembles Disneyland or Disney World. There's a big poster of Walt Disney with the word VISION and one of my favorite quotes from him—"It's kind of fun to do the impossible." There's a wall full of Walt Disney photos and quotes all around. And there's a section of books just about Disney. I think I've read everything written by or about Walt Disney.

I wasn't much of a reader through high school and college, but

I became absolutely voracious when I got into the baseball business. Knowledge really is power. I started *inhaling* books—and I couldn't get enough of Walt Disney.

Disney is my jam.

I've had some good Disney moments. Emily surprised me with a trip to the Walt Disney family museum in San Francisco. I got together with the author of *Walt Disney's Way*, a book about Walt's marketing instincts, and we spent two days at Disney World going through the intricacies of EPCOT and the Magic Kingdom. Those were two brilliant, magical days.

My Disney fascination started when I was eight years old. My father and I got on a plane, but I didn't know where we were going until I heard the announcement:

"We will be landing in Orlando shortly."

My eyes got big and I turned to my dad: "We're going to Disney?" I was so excited. Every day, we were strategic, going to the park early so we could get on as many rides as possible.

One day, we arrived before the park opened and visited Typhoon Lagoon, and a cast member said, "All right, it's now time to find our Big Kahuna for the day. Whoever gets the answers to our trivia questions will be the Big Kahuna." I didn't even know what the Big Kahuna was, but I knew I wanted to be one.

They asked questions like, "How high does the water go off the ship at Typhoon Lagoon?" and "How much water do we use?" I watched a ten-year-old kid win, and they gave him a big medallion. Then he went into the park before it opened to everyone else.

I begged my dad to let me go back a couple of days later. I wanted to be the Big Kahuna. I had studied a brochure on Typhoon Lagoon, and this time, I nailed every question. When they gave me the medallion, it was still thirty minutes until they opened the gates. So it was like the park opened just for me. I went down every slide. It was the time of my life, the best thing ever. It was my first bit of Disney magic.

And yes, I still have that Big Kahuna medallion.

Disney has always been special to me, even to this day. Just a few years ago, Emily and I went to EPCOT on our first book tour. When we pulled up, the woman saw me in my yellow tuxedo and Emily pregnant. She handed us a parking pass and said, "Have a magical day. This one's on me." We didn't have to pay. It's just tiny things like that that make parkgoers realize Disney is unique and that its people—Disney calls its employees cast members—are empowered to create special moments.

We want the Bananas to represent the same thing. How can we make that work? Well, when I noticed an upset boy standing in a line outside Grayson Stadium, I went over to investigate. His parents explained they had been late and the boy missed a chance to march in the Little League parade before our Bananas game. I turned to the boy, probably about eight years old, and said, "Come with me." I grabbed one of our players, introduced him to the child, and they played catch on the field for ten minutes. The boy was so excited. I could see the father and mother beaming in the stands. We don't want any red tape with the Bananas. We always want to create those magical memories for fans. Our staff is empowered to do things like this all the time.

We now have our "Bananas Kings of the Game." We pick three kids—all about five or six years old—and they have one minute to get high fives from the crowd and have it make as much noise as possible. Whoever gets the most high fives wins. And every night, I say it's too close to pick one winner, so all three of them are given crowns to wear.

So the kids get treated like a king—or a Big Kahuna.

I wear Walt Disney's mission on my sleeve, so people always wonder what would've happened if I ever had met him. I think I'd just want to walk around his park with him. I'd ask about the things I saw or smelled. I'd probably drive him crazy, picking his brain. But I'd love to know more about his attention to detail.

For Disney, every concept led to something bigger. He called it "plussing." He never shot down ideas. If someone criticized something, the person was expected to "plus" it: come up with a new idea or strengthen the original thought. We've adopted that with the Bananas. Every experiment feeds into something else.

The evolution of Disney's company was truly amazing. It went from drawing the animations to a full-length animated film. It went from synchronized sounds to full color and then a full-length animated film. Disney's business evolved from a small art studio to a huge studio in Burbank. Then he went from building Disneyland to Disney World, then to creating the city of tomorrow, the EPCOT he never got to see.

I'm so taken with everything that Walt Disney stood for that I did book reports on the key things that were written about him. Repeat: book reports. I did these as an adult who wanted to absorb information, not as a student who was trying to get a good grade. I read and reread the books constantly, but I also refer often to the takeaways in my book reports.

I doubt whether one person in fifty million is capable of the obsessive focus with which Walt lived every day of his life. And it was not in any way a selfish obsession. He was not focused on making money or acquiring fame, although he did both. His grand obsession was simply to bring happiness to others. That was his total focus. It made Walt Disney who he was.

I did a similar report with a book on P. T. Barnum: *There's A Customer Born Every Minute.*

The idea behind publicity stunts is to get attention. It's no longer enough to advertise or hand out flyers or sit at a trade show. You have to think more outrageously and act more boldly, and you have to deliver what you promise, or else. . . . What could we show at the ballpark or have that doesn't make any sense? Have fans see something different. Person coaching first base on stilts, or a contortionist. Players entering the field on a trash truck—taking out the trash. Coaches riding a horse. Bananas parade coming through town during our Road Shows. . . . By thinking of the concept of contrast, you can start to brainstorm ways to grab attention for your own business. Imagine something so different, so bizarre, so unusual—something bigger or better than what people see every day—and you grab attention. The secret is contrast.

P. T. Barnum was the greatest marketer of all time with what he did in the 1800s. I can't imagine what he would have done with social media. It would be a hundred times wilder than the Bananas. And it's crazy to think about something bigger than us because we have guys who come up with bats on fire, players on stilts, people doing splits at home plate.

If P. T. Barnum was running TikTok, you'd witness huge spectacles. I mean, to attract customers, he had an elephant on his property next to the railroad tracks. He tried to acquire the most unique, creative talent and do things no one else in the world was doing. The world's first, the world's biggest, the world's tallest pitcher . . . that's all very P. T. Barnum–inspired. He was fascinating. He would do anything to create attention.

Of course, I'm also inspired by Bill Veeck, the longtime major-league owner of various teams, including the White Sox. Where to start with *that* guy? He was the most fans-first owner of all time. I mean, the exploding scoreboard, the names on the backs of jerseys, sending three-foot-seven Eddie Gaedel up to the plate, Disco Demolition Night, you name it. He gave twelve live lobsters to a fan during a game just to see what would happen. He had a million ideas and wasn't hesitant to shake things up.

When I was Gastonia's general manager, Ken sent me to a conference, and that's where I came across Mike Veeck, Bill's son, another baseball innovator. As everyone else was getting ready for lunch, I approached Mike Veeck.

"Mike, I need some advice. I just took over a team that's failing. There are no fans coming. What do I do?"

My tone was urgent.

Mike just stared at me and said, "Well, I can sense your enthusiasm." He told me I had to be the face of the team. Then he added, "And you've got to get a little crazy. That's all."

I thanked him and walked away. And that's when my mind really began racing. I realized I needed to get out there in front of people, so I started coming up with crazy ideas.

The Grandma Beauty Pageant. Flatulence Fun Night. Dig to China Night. We fired our mascot for HGH (human growth hormone) use, but we called it BGH because he was a bear. We offered President Bush an internship with the team because his term was up. When we announced on April Fool's Day that he had accepted the job, we were getting calls from people who wanted tickets so they could meet the former president.

The trick was finding ways to get attention. The path to success was constantly coming up with ideas. It was whatever I could do to stand out—and that is still what we do today.

I have understood that part from the beginning of my tenure in college summer-league baseball.

After I got promoted from intern at Gastonia, Ken let me follow through on my ideas. He empowered me as much as anybody has ever been empowered.

The interactions between Ken and me must have been funny to watch. I would bounce in with my latest idea. And Ken always humored me, nodding his head and going, "OK, hmmm, interesting."

I once promised Ken we were going to have our best night ever—Midnight Madness. We would start the game at midnight and lead up to it with all these crazy promotions. It was going to be great!

Ken later said he was thinking to himself, *That is the dumbest idea I've ever heard in my life. We can't get people there at eight o'clock, let alone midnight. But I can't step on this guy's toes. I gave him the job. Now I have to let him run with it a little bit.*

We had bed races. We had home run derbies. We had pillow fights on the field. The night was absolutely insane. We basically sold it out.

Ken, shocked and amazed by these proceedings, said he knew then I was the right guy to make Gastonia baseball into a business success.

Back then we also had trouble drawing fans on Sundays. North Carolina, after all, was in the Bible Belt. It just never worked. I proposed a Community Give Back Night with free admission for everyone. Not only that, but we would feed the first one thousand people, which was more than we'd draw for a normal Sunday game.

Ken just stared at me but gave a thumbs-up to that one, too. He told me later he had no idea what I was thinking. But we sold sponsorships, and local companies paid for giveaways of televisions, furniture, restaurant gift cards, and, my personal favorite, a year's supply of Moe's burritos.

Ken got to the stadium about two o'clock for a game that would start at five. There was a line of people around the stadium, even then. When the fans entered, they were basically kissing Ken's feet and thanking him for putting on such an event because it helped so many people. He was quick to say he'd really had nothing to do with it. He had just given me permission to do it. That night was a huge home run—four thousand fans in all—and it created big-time goodwill in Gastonia.

There are plenty of classic stories. But strangely, I can't pinpoint a definitive moment I had with Ken, a singular thing he told me that made a huge difference, when he truly shared his soul and I felt my life change. Actually, the biggest difference was Ken's consistency. I had a constant role model, somebody who owned minor-league teams, had a career of success, and made a life for himself and his family.

I could always say to him, "Hey, I've got an idea." Or, "Here's what I've been thinking about." And I wouldn't be laughed out of the building. Ken and I are different people. He's a numbers guy, a business guy. I'm just this person with constantly crazy ideas, but Ken always encouraged them by pushing the right buttons. I think about Walt Disney and his older brother, Roy, who often served as the encouraging adviser and business manager. That allowed Walt to fully pursue his creative ventures. Ken was my Roy for my first ten-plus years in baseball.

If I proposed things, even if they didn't look promising or profitable, Ken found a way to say yes. He believed in what Emily and I wanted to do. Meanwhile, I also leaned on my ghost mentors—Walt Disney, P. T. Barnum, and Bill Veeck—who taught me about showmanship, attracting attention, and having fun. But Ken clearly put me in position to make things happen.

Ken, in his typical way, always deflected any praise when I described him as my mentor.

"Jesse knows how to get people into the ballpark," Ken said. "The way he approached everything was just so different than anybody else. I've been doing this for nearly forty years—a long, long time. He just does things differently. He sees things others don't see."

Well, with whatever success we have, I'm always giving Ken plenty of credit. Those nights in the Jeep Grand Cherokee were invaluable. It really was like taking a graduate course. He taught me about running a baseball team, family, and life.

That's still my foundation. And as we began our new life in Savannah, and were about to get tested like never before, we knew we'd need to lean on our mentors more than ever.

Chapter Nine

The Name and the Look

The Savannah Bananas?

I immediately *loved* the name. I can't explain how much I loved the name. It started with a Name the Team contest we ran through the *Savannah Morning News*, which received more than one thousand entries.

One of our very first entries was from a woman in Savannah named Lynn Moses, who suggested "Savannah Bananas." She was the only one who suggested the name; more about Lynn later on.

About a month out, we had narrowed the entries to five— Bananas, Anchors, Ports, Seagulls, and Party Animals. For our big reveal on February 25, 2016, we were down to three finalists— Bananas, Anchors, and Ports.

Honestly, in my mind, none of the other names had a chance. I can't remember which one came in second—personally, Party Animals was my number two—but Bananas was clearly first. By a mile.

The Savannah Bananas. It sounded awesome, and it rhymed.

I immediately thought about the potential of the brand and how we could make it stand out and be different. "Let's Go Bananas!"—it was a natural.

Look, you name teams after fierce animals. Team names are supposed to sound intimidating. Fruit isn't intimidating. Naming a team after fruit—it's just not done. It's not a smart move for a sporting business.

But remember who we are. We're different. We look at what everyone else does—then we do the opposite.

In the original *Morning News* article that announced our contest, I stressed that we wanted something unique. To me, "Savannah Bananas" was absolute perfection. I wish I could say everyone else in town shared my enthusiasm.

You all should be fired.

Throw the owner out of town.

This is the worst name we've ever heard of.

And those were some of the more gentle reactions.

Initially the criticism got to me. Maybe at least in part because we were so invested. When Emily and I visited Grayson Stadium after getting engaged, we fell in love with the place. We knew then, if we ever had the opportunity to own a team, we'd like it to be in Savannah.

Then we got that chance. We were so excited, we could hardly sleep at night. And we were told from day one that we were going to fail.

At first, we did just that. We sold only a handful of tickets in the preseason. It was bad. Emily and I were just kids trying to prove ourselves in a bigger market, and we were getting shut down every day. Whether it was sponsorships, tickets, or just getting people interested in being involved with us, we had nothing. Nothing.

That's when we made the decision to go all-in on fun. Once we had our name, we clarified our identity. We had, I thought, the absolute perfect team name. In fact, maybe the greatest team name in the history of team names, and the most fun.

And then? I hadn't counted on such an angry initial reaction. But it also was another indication that I have the greatest wife in the world. Emily was the rock.

"Emily, what is going on here?" I said. "Why are so many people against this team name? This is just brutal."

Emily reassured me like a mom would do to a kid on the first day of school.

"Jesse, this team name is exactly what we need," Emily said. "No one else has one like it. We just have to get them to experience it, and they will love it just like you do. Everything is going to be just fine."

I give Emily full credit: she saw the future. When we first picked the name, I was over-the-moon excited. Emily was extra cautious.

"Look, we're going to get a lot of criticism," Emily told me before the flood of negative reactions began. "We've got to make sure our team is prepared to handle that."

"What are you talking about?" I said. "It's a *great* name."

"I completely agree, but I also think I know how people think, so we better be ready," Emily said as she pulled out a piece of paper and a pen.

"What are you writing?" I said.

"Our strategy," Emily said. "You'll see."

Emily wrote down a series of questions—and they were all confrontational.

Where did you come up with such a stupid name?
Why are you being so silly? How can we take you seriously?
Who thought of this nonsense? I'm not going to support this
team.

Our staff was very young and impressionable. So Emily set up
a series of role-playing exercises. She acted like she was a telephone caller—she even said "Ring! Ring!"—and one of our staffers acted like they had just answered the telephone.

Then Emily shouted in a very angry voice:

"That is the stupidest name I've ever heard. Y'all should be
ashamed of yourself. Who came up with that anyway?"

After some practice, our staffers knew exactly how to handle
any potential objections. Our mantra to the staff was simple:
Stay positive. Stay the course. Remember, this is a vocal minority.
So I practiced a response for them:

"Well, first of all, thanks for calling. We appreciate your interest in our team. We wanted our team name to be unique and
special, kind of like the city of Savannah itself. We wanted to be
different than all those other teams, and we wanted to be fun."

This went on for a few hours. If one of our staffers didn't have
an answer for the complaints or felt panicked over being attacked,
we coached them up until they felt comfortable.

Then, as our big team name reveal got closer and closer, the
anxiety levels hit a fever pitch with our staff.

"It's going to be OK, guys," Emily said. "Remember, we've got
a whole bunch of ringers."

Ringers?

That's right. We had a few waves of ringers coming to the
reveal—family, friends, local supporters, anybody we could think
of who would give us about a hundred or so people going abso-

lutely over-the-top, enthusiastically crazy when "Savannah Bananas" first went public. If everybody was cheering in the room, there was a good chance that any on-the-fence fans would be swayed to the positive side.

But the whole event was shaping up like a disaster.

We had a stage in front of the concession stand, and we were going to show a video to the crowd. The only problem? We didn't know how to make a really good video.

Alex McDonald, Emily's brother (yes, the same brother who was overseeing our financials), stayed up all night making that video because we wanted to show everyone all the fun we had had with the Gastonia Grizzlies. We wondered if he could get it ready in time.

We never got the shipment of hats that we needed for our reveal press conference. And we had to put a rush order so we could get T-shirts. Our first shipment of shirts had *Bananas* misspelled—it was *B-A-N-N-A-N-A-S*. Wow! True story.

We were launching our team name with no hats and replacement shirts. It was chaotic.

A few hundred people *were* there for the announcement, including a full complement of television stations, radio stations, and newspaper reporters.

And when we finally said . . . Savannah Bananas . . . the reaction *was* crazy.

There *was* wild cheering, but only from our ringers, not anyone else.

Some people were booing.

I think most of the others were just in utter shock.

I saw lots of people going to our merchandise store to buy T-shirts. That all looked good. I hardly had time to get discouraged.

While I was still trying to absorb everything, Emily rushed

over and breathlessly said, "Jesse, you wouldn't believe what's happening!"

People were buying the T-shirts and hats, even though we wouldn't get the actual hats for about four months. They were so rabid, they bought the hats based solely on what was portrayed on our website. Orders were coming in left and right. We didn't have a system or process to handle that volume. It was utter chaos. We couldn't even catch our breath to figure it out.

Within thirty minutes, "Savannah Bananas" was the number one trending topic on Twitter. We live in a warp-speed world these days. Once "Savannah Bananas" got out into cyberspace, it practically broke the Internet. All over the country—all over the world—people were buzzing about our name and our look. The neon yellow coloring, the green outline, the cool lettering, the logo with the gritty-looking banana swinging a bat, I'm telling you, it was an instant sensation.

But then the local media started putting out their stories. The negative vibes kept coming and coming. And the comments from readers and viewers followed that. Some of them were absolute gut punches.

You'll never sell a ticket.

You guys are an embarrassment to the city.

You're going to need to give away tickets to help the morale of this team.

I was losing my mind.

"Jesse, this is exactly what we wanted," Emily said. "It's what we talked about. We're getting attention. We practiced how to react to this. We actually practiced it. Remember?"

"Yeah, I remember," I said. "But now that it's actually happening, it's brutal. It's like we're getting ripped apart."

Here's the crazy thing: the Savannah media was very critical, and it seemed like everyone in town was against us. But nationally, it was different. ESPN's *SportsCenter* reached out and gave us a great shout-out. We were at Coach's Corner, a sports bar, and all of a sudden we saw our Savannah Bananas logo up on the screen. Underneath, it said, "Logo of the Year?" We were yelling at the top of our lungs. This was a very big deal for a bunch of kids running a college summer baseball team in Savannah, Georgia.

Still, I barely slept that night. My mind was racing. The anxiety started creeping in.

"Emily, what have we gotten ourselves into?" I said. "What's going to happen next? Emily? Emily?"

She was asleep, tired from trying to hold it together all day.

We were sleeping on one of those double air mattresses, and I wore socks because the floors were so disgusting in our apartment. When I went to the bathroom, then plopped back down on the air mattress, Emily practically went airborne. I mean, the whole thing was insane. It was something out of a bad situation comedy.

I continued to torture myself and read all the comments. I couldn't help it. I had to know what the people were saying.

"Emily, listen to these things," I said, refusing to let Emily stay asleep. "They're calling me a demented Willy Wonka character."

"Well, you know, that is kind of funny," Emily said, chuckling.

"That is *not* funny," I said.

No response. I wanted sympathy. I needed an audience.

"What have we gotten ourselves into, Emily?" I said, wailing a little bit.

"Jesse . . . good night," Emily said, pretty much exhausted at that point.

They always say things look better in the morning, right? That was true for us, too. I was hypersensitive to all the comments, but there were bright spots everywhere, too. Savannah Bananas merchandise went on sale immediately after we announced the team name. If the Gastonia Grizzlies had sales of $1,000 in one game for merchandise, we said, "Oh my God!" Like it was unbelievable. Our biggest year in merchandise at Gastonia was $20,000—total. That was my context.

We did $20,000 in Bananas merchandise in the first couple of days after announcing the team name. And in a few years, those numbers went from staggering to downright unbelievable. Our summer college team's merchandise sales grew to double that of the bestselling minor-league team—a team that played thirty or forty more games than us and by definition was filled with pros. That still amazes me.

I talk to minor-league operators, and they've just laughed at our numbers because they can't believe what they're hearing. I could never have imagined the sales, and it's not about the merchandise sales—which is now into eight figures annually—it's about the quality of our brand and how much people love it.

We've seen pictures of people wearing Bananas gear outside the Colosseum in Rome, scaling mountains, and on every cruise ship known to man. We've seen fans posting photos to Facebook and Instagram of themselves wearing Bananas shirts at all major sporting events.

By 2022, we were doing more in merchandise alone than we

had during our biggest previous year ever at Savannah, including tickets, merchandise, food, and everything.

And it all started back when Lynn Moses submitted "Savannah Bananas."

I thought Jared, our team president, had a pretty nice perspective on the birth of the Bananas:

"When we first got to Savannah, no one trusted us," Jared said. "Everyone thought our organization would be a fly-by-night operation. We had nothing. The city had been told that baseball is dead in Savannah. We walked into waves and waves of negativity.

"To think that six years later, in 2022, we would have played in front of hundreds of thousands of fans in Savannah; then we had a World Tour, where we played before sixty thousand fans in six different cities that we had never been to before. We were in America's oldest professional ballpark—Rickwood Field in Birmingham—and played at the spring training facility of two major-league world champion teams in West Palm Beach. How does that come together?"

It's bananas!

There's that word again.

The word that helped us to think creatively and discover the new world of Bananaland—throwing out the first banana, the Banana Baby (a fan's baby we celebrate on the field à la *The Lion King*), the Banana-Nanas (grandma dance team), the Man-Nanas (dad-bod cheerleading squad), Split (our mascot), the song "Can't Stop the Peeling," and every other wild and wacky dream as our future continues to ripen.

Usually, once ownership decides on a name, it announces it and introduces a logo. People react to it, and that's about it. There are very few instances where you can build a long-lasting brand. The reality is we have ideas we haven't even touched yet. Our brand inspires new ideas constantly.

The Savannah Bananas.

So how did it all begin? That's where we come back to Lynn Moses. She's a local, Savannah's Jenkins High School, class of 1970. In fact, her class graduated at Grayson Stadium, the Bananas' home field. She earned her sociology degree at Valdosta State in Georgia. When her children began school, she completed her nursing degree at Armstrong State in Georgia, then worked at Savannah's Candler Hospital for thirty-four years.

As Lynn tells it, she was a regular on the night shift. So she was accustomed to staying up late and perusing the Internet. She looked forward to the postmidnight hours because that's when the *Savannah Morning News* would post its stories for the next day.

"I saw an announcement for a contest to name a summer college baseball team that was going to play at Grayson Stadium," Lynn said. "It said they were going to be a different kind of team and they wanted a family-friendly mascot.

"In my mind, I saw this picture of a banana—a smiling banana mascot, almost like a skinny, spinning banana. I remember thinking, *Well, I don't think college boys want to be known as bananas*. But it sounded friendly and kind of silly. I mean, the Savannah Bananas? Oh, why not? It was the first day of the contest, and I entered it. I got an email thanking me for entering, then another one a few days later trying to sell me season tickets. But I ignored that and just kind of forgot about it all."

Flash forward another month or so.

The *Morning News* published the top five entries.

"I showed it to my daughter and said, 'My entry is one of the five!'" Lynn said. "And my daughter said, 'Oh, I hope it's not the Savannah Bananas.' We just laughed and, again, I didn't think anything more about it."

We contacted Lynn to tell her "Bananas" was among our top three choices and we wanted her to come to our reveal. She said she couldn't because she had to work that night.

I called Lynn up and wasn't taking no for an answer.

"Lynn, you need to come because it's going to be so much fun and you have one of the names that's being considered," I said.

"Well, that's nice, and I appreciate it, but I have to work," Lynn said, trying to get me off the phone. "I have to be at the hospital by six forty-five. I just can't make it. I'm sorry."

"You don't have to stay long," I said. "We'll have food and drinks. You can have supper with us, have a little fun, and we'll make sure you get to work on time. Please? It's going to be really great. I promise. Please?"

Obviously, we wanted Lynn to come—hint, hint—so I talked her into it. When we officially unveiled the Savannah Bananas, Lynn was escorted to the podium wearing her full nursing uniform. I think she was shocked.

"My family was there and they took pictures," Lynn said. "I don't remember much. It was kind of a blur. I was thinking, *Don't embarrass yourself*, but I can't even remember what I said. They gave me two season tickets and some T-shirts.

"The next day, it seemed like everybody was hating on the name. I felt so bad. My brothers were sending me things from the Internet and saying, 'You're famous!' And I'm like, 'But everybody hates the name.' I had no idea how big this was going to get. That night at work, somebody brought in a banana bread dessert and on the top was written, 'Go Bananas!' What do they always say? And the rest is history."

Lynn and her husband, Gary, became some of our most devoted Bananas fans. When Lynn retired from Candler Hospital, she put in for her last official workday. When she realized the Bananas played that night, she changed the date. She didn't want to miss a game. Right after attending the final Bananas game of 2021, Gary Moses got sick with COVID and unfortunately passed away. Lynn said Gary was probably the biggest Bananas fan in their family. He loved bragging to fans that his wife had come up with the team's name.

"It's different going to games without him, but I'm glad we had that last summer together and had a ball watching the Bananas," Lynn said. "It's still fun. I'm proud that Savannah has such an event and everybody wants to come to our town to see it.

"I'm amused by it. It feels like everyone can go there and forget about their worries. The happiness in that stadium is just contagious. How many places can you go these days to feel like that? It's amazing, and I don't think I've stopped smiling since that first night when I looked up on that screen and saw the Savannah Bananas logo. How can you not smile when you see that?"

That was the idea.

After Lynn suggested the name and before we revealed our decision, we had to come up with the right colors and logo. The logo had to be perfect, and I definitely think we knocked it out of the park.

For that, I give credit to Dan Simon, one of the nation's top sports design and branding artists. He is based in Louisville and came highly recommended after we asked around to other teams that had unveiled new logos. Dan has done a lot of branding for teams in minor-league baseball, put together some events for the major leagues and even created a couple of Super Bowl logos.

We've never heard one negative comment about our logo, which is amazing. When any team launches a brand, there are always people who don't like the name, and a good percentage of people will say that the logo is stupid, that the colors are stupid, that it's all dumb, and they say they will refuse to wear it.

There were about eight weeks between the close of our Name the Team contest and the unveiling of our logo. To get a feel for what I wanted for the team, Dan spent a month just talking to me. I would say, "Hey, if you've got time on your calendar, I'd like to talk to you a bit." So we'd talk for an hour. He asked deep and probing questions about the character of the banana I wanted, as well as the color schemes and how we wanted people to feel when they saw it.

The one thing I kept saying—and I don't use this language much—but I told Dan it had to be a "badass banana." I didn't want anything wimpy. I wanted Banana people to be proud to wear it. And I knew I wanted our colors to be in tropical tones, so people could feel like they were on vacation when they came to our games.

When the Bananas' name came out, I remember thinking, *We're going to have to talk to the players to make them feel like they aren't playing for a wimpy little fruit.* I think the branding and design took care of that. It's a cool-looking uniform.

I remember asking Dan, "How many different renderings do we get?"

And Dan said, "You get one."

I was pretty surprised.

Dan said he wouldn't miss it. In fact, he said, "It will be exactly what you want."

And I thought to myself, *No way. How's he going to do that? All we've done is talk. We'll have to tweak and adjust it.*

Then the first time when he sent the logo, I sat there, looked at it, and thought, *Wow!* It was perfect. It was exactly what we wanted. And it's exactly as it is right now.

How did Dan Simon do it so well?

"Crazy names, goofy names, silly names have become de rigueur in the minor-league arena . . . and some of them, I think, go a bit too far," Dan said. "They don't take into consideration they have to be worn by athletes playing at a high level and those athletes shouldn't be embarrassed by what they are wearing.

"When Jesse came to me, they were still considering the various team names. But when he told me 'Savannah Bananas,' I immediately got an ear-to-ear smile on my face. And I told him, 'Jesse, you're crazy if you don't go with that name.' I thought it was perfect."

But Dan said he wasn't as sure about our situation in Savannah. With his experience in minor-league baseball, he knew about how the affiliated teams had struggled through the years in Savannah. When we came to him about a logo for a college summer-league team, Dan later said he felt bad about taking our money. All that being said, it wasn't his job to speculate on whether the Bananas would work in Savannah. He had been hired to produce a logo and a color scheme.

"I ask a lot of questions, and I do a lot of listening," Dan said. "Having done this for a long time, I know the right questions to ask. I have the ability to hear those words and turn them into visual images. So you anthropomorphize the banana—giving it human characteristics—and I created my own typography that suggested baseball script.

"And here's maybe the most important part of creating this identity. If you take a silly name and give an equally silly visual representation, then you've gone the wrong direction. You give it a visual *attitude*. That combination, those ingredients, when mixed together, it produces a flavor that people just want to eat up."

It's cool to see how popular our merchandise has become.

In 2020, the staff from the Amazon Prime thriller series *Reacher* reached out and asked for two Savannah Bananas T-shirts. The series is based in Georgia, and a lead character wore the shirts on the next episode. We had been getting a few dozen orders a day for those particular shirts. It immediately went up to hundreds a day.

At our home games, our merchandise shop is fully stocked. By the end of the night, most of it is gone.

We have consulted with Eric Sundvold, an assistant buyer with Legends Global Merchandise, a retail and merchandising giant that was started by the New York Yankees and Dallas Cowboys. Eric said he now considers the Savannah Bananas logo to be iconic.

"It's all over the country now, and it's going to be all over the world eventually," Eric said. "The branding is phenomenal. It's genius. Everything is geared toward the fan. The coloring is great, and the neon green makes it stand out even more.

"What an incredibly inspired name—the Savannah Bananas. It's a funny thing to say, and it plays into the fun the team wants to bring. Savannah's market has taken hits for not being able to support a team. I think the market just wasn't being played properly. Right now, I see no other team in the country that plays to their market like the Savannah Bananas. The whole thing has been a merchandising and marketing phenomenon. It has been executed perfectly, starting with the selection of the name itself."

The Savannah Bananas.

We're grateful for Lynn Moses, whose late-night vision of the "Savannah Bananas" set in motion our destiny. We will remember her forever.

"I gave them the little seed that got planted—and it grew really big," Lynn said. "Everything kind of spun off my silly idea for a team name. Sometimes, the way things happen in life is really, really funny, almost unexplainable. All you can do is laugh."

Chapter Ten

Birth of the Bananas

Every company these days has a mission statement, right? With the Savannah Bananas, our mission is pretty simple. It was established on day one.

Fans First. Entertain Always.

And we're all-in on fun.

The story of the Bananas' beginning has been told so much, it almost has a life of its own. But it's true. After buying the team in Savannah, where baseball had never worked, Emily and I were down to our last few dollars. Nobody believed in us. We could barely get people to return our telephone calls. We were $1.8 million in debt. We were sleeping on an air mattress.

Our place was located on Tybee Island, which sounds really exotic. But it had dropped in value about $100,000, and it had been on the market for three years. Calling it a fixer-upper would have been charitable. That place, though, was in perfect sync with our personalities. We usually go opposite from the way other people would go. I guess we're attracted to old houses, old stadiums, and other things where people don't see the value. We don't see what things are. We see what things can be. That's true in everything we do.

So with baseball, we knew we had to do something different. I mean, something dramatically different. That's when we reminded ourselves what business we were really in—the entertainment business.

But what kind of business strips all the advertising signage off its outfield walls and gives up thousands of dollars in revenue? We did this in 2020, just before the COVID-19 pandemic. We had hundreds of thousands of dollars in sponsorships. Although it wasn't a large part of our overall revenue, it was something. It had never been done in the industry. I don't know if it will ever be done again. It was shocking to a lot of people, but we decided that we didn't want to get people in the stadium for a sales opportunity. That wasn't part of our fan experience.

What kind of business doesn't charge for parking and includes all-you-can eat food and drinks in the ticket price?

What kind of business has free shipping for its merchandise, even throwing in free koozies and cookies all in a yellow custom box?

That's us. That's the Savannah Bananas. We're a fans-first business—all the way. We don't make decisions based on revenue. We believe that if we build a loyal fan base, the rest takes care of itself.

When we played our first game as a college summer-league team in 2016, we wore green uniforms. Get it? We weren't quite ripe. Well, it rained and rained and rained. We were delayed for two hours and didn't get started until 8:30.

We did all kinds of crazy things, like dancing in the rain, and holding banana-style games, such as blindfolding a fan, dropping a banana somewhere in the infield, and having them crawl around to find it, listening to the crowd's cheers or boos for direction hints. We would try anything to keep the people entertained. The fans didn't want to leave. We definitely played like we weren't ripe. We made six errors and lost the game. But people went home and told their friends, "You have to see this. This is something different."

We never looked back. From that point on, we sold out every game. Our waiting list for tickets grew into the thousands. And it's all because we represent fans-first entertainment.

Here's what I don't understand about many businesses. Why do they continually do the things that their customers hate? Why are people endlessly put on hold, while a message plays that tells them how "important" their call is, but they do a slow burn while waiting to talk to an actual human being . . . and maybe they still hang up in frustration?

In the Bananas' organization, we have a word for this— *friction*.

We looked at all the friction points from a baseball experience— ticket fees, price gouging on parking and concessions, as well as limited access to autographs and fan photos with their favorite players—and we did the opposite.

Before reaching the point of innovation, we had to find the friction points of the fan experience. We had to put ourselves in the fans' shoes. Are the fans treated well? Is the website easy to navigate? Are fans' concerns and complaints solved promptly? Every paying point is a pain point, so are the prices fair? Or are your fans being nickel-and-dimed to death?

On the field, we eliminated long, slow, and boring. Off the field, we listened to the fans. Because if we want raving fans, the most loyal advocates we could imagine, the best business model in the world is simply this:

Stop. Doing. What. They. Hate.

Once we eliminated the friction, then we experimented to create an empowered, engaging team.

When people say "customer service," I cringe. I hate the word *customer* and so I switch it to *fans*. To me, *customer* suggests some sort of transaction. Customers come and go. Fans never leave. They are fired up, glad to be there. With the Bananas, every question we have begins with this: Is it Fans First?

We walk around our ballpark and talk to fans. Once we're in their shoes, we understand how they feel and how they want to be treated.

From time to time, I'll go undercover at our games because that's where I can learn. The first time I did that, I went to park and my car bottomed out on a pothole. As I walked in, our parking penguins (what we call our parking attendants) had their backs to me and were eating burgers. Those were things I did not want to see, so I immediately reminded our staff of the expectations.

A lot of times, owners don't know the little details, but those little details matter. Everything speaks. A little pothole demonstrates little care about the parking lot. I feel that trash on the ground, even a half mile from your ballpark, demonstrates ownership doesn't care. We are actually that obsessed with making it an ideal experience.

We don't do surveys. I don't believe in them. We learn everything by watching fans. People speak more with their actions than their words. How are the fans reacting? When we do a promotion, we look for smiles and laughter.

When George Lucas created *Star Wars*, his goal was to create a movie that he would love. That's our goal, too. We're trying to create a fan experience that we would love. If we're bored by something, there's a good chance that the fans will be bored, too.

What I've come to realize is the Savannah Bananas have hit a nerve. I think we found what the fans were starving for—fun.

We have lots of allies in this philosophy. Two guys who completely get it are Jake Peavy, a former Cy Young Award winner, and Eric Byrnes, our Bananas head coach during our first World Tour. They both played at the highest levels in the big leagues. They have made a lot of money, won awards, and done things on the field that others can only dream about. They also know how much fans matter.

"If somebody wants to hate on what the Bananas are doing? Get out of here," Jake said. "There's nothing to hate here. Why isn't there more of this throughout baseball? I understand that the game has to be serious, but people go to the ballpark for entertainment. It's fun to watch the best ballplayers in the world. But it's also fun to see some antics. They want fun walk-up songs and personality and showmanship. It's OK for people to have fun. The world has enough cruel and evil things in it. Fun is OK."

Byrnesie (that's the nickname everyone has for Eric Byrnes) not only played but he also worked at the MLB Network. He knows his stuff. For too long, he says, baseball believed that its product alone won the day. Fans could take it or leave it.

"Now there's a growing disconnect," Byrnesie said. "I don't think the product alone plays anymore. It's too slow. You've got to take care of your fans and show them that they matter. Players have always been trained and conditioned to think all they have to do is perform on the field. A part of that is true. But for the whole sport to move forward, a lot has to change. The lifeblood of baseball is building a relationship with fans. It's a huge mistake to be arrogant and think that's not the case. The whole experience has to be fun."

With the Bananas, our fans have fun, but so do our players and staff.

When people leave our ballpark, we want them to say, "Wow! That was the most fun I've ever had at a baseball stadium." Was it the most competitive game of baseball ever? Doubtful. But it can be the most fun and fastest game they've ever seen.

And it can be surrounded with so much entertainment that it's hard to know where to start.

The Bananas have a ten-piece pep band. We have a princess and a magician. We have a break-dancing first-base coach. Even our home-plate umpire dances sometimes—who twerks and does ridiculous strikeout dances. We have the Banana-Nanas, our senior-citizen dance team, and the Man-Nanas, our dad-bod cheerleading squad. We have a DJ who continually pumps in the music. And I'm usually right in the middle of it all, with my yellow top hat and tuxedo, singing, dancing, setting up stunts, and throwing beads to the crowd like it's Mardi Gras.

Some people have called the Bananas a straight-up challenge to baseball's traditions. What's usually found at ball games? Usually, there's soft organ music. Why *not* a pep band, especially one that can march around the stadium and get fans involved? When our band enters, we can see the faces light up. We've heard the fans say, "Oh my gosh! There's a band at a baseball game?" They're shocked, but they love it.

How about a princess?

Our Princess Potassia is Hannah Elizabeth Smith, who started with us while she did her performing arts graduate program at the Savannah College of Art and Design. Our princess is always in character.

Fan: Who are you really?

Princess: I'm Princess Potassia. I'm heir to the throne of Bananaland. One day, I will be a queen.

Fan: Where are you from?

Princess: From Bananaland. I was born in a banana blossom.

Fan: How did you get this job?

Princess: Well, I was born a princess.

Perfect.

Princess Potassia begins with a victory song—she rewrote the lyrics from a tune in Disney's movie *Tangled*. She tries to be gentle and accessible, while making the children feel safe. For some of the younger ones, the noise and fireworks are scary. The princess is a comforting character, and she's a welcome sight for young girls, some of whom may have been dragged to baseball games with their brothers. They might think a Bananas game is another boring thing they have to endure, but they practically shriek at the sight of a princess. To them, princesses can do anything.

"Who expects to see a princess at a baseball game?" Hannah said. "It's so unique. I want Princess Potassia to be mysterious. I'll see people in a store and they'll say, 'I know you from somewhere. Wait, I think I saw you at the ballpark!' And I'll just leave the mystery there. 'Yes, I think you did.' They know. I know they know. Just keep it a mystery, a novelty. It's different."

Speaking of different things, how about our Banana-Nanas? Now *that* is something fans wouldn't expect—local ladies, anywhere from sixty-five to eighty years old, dancing to some hip-hop and shaking their stuff.

"It doesn't matter how old we are—we know how to move it,"

said Banana-Nana Gail Case. "I've seen people come here and say, 'Oh, this is so ridiculous.' Well, that's the point—being ridiculous.

"I think the Nanas surprise people. We're not skinny little girls. Like Cyndi Lauper said, 'Girls Just Wanna Have Fun' . . . at any age. Really, we are like the Laker Girls or the Dallas Cowboy Cheerleaders. Same moves, but we're wearing more clothes."

Another surprise, and certainly not skinny: the dad-bod cheerleading squad. For fans who are accustomed to athletic females dancing on the dugouts, we offer a team of out-of-shape men wearing wigs and kilts. But they have spirit.

"It's probably a shock to see us walk out there," dad-bod stalwart Tris Meyers said. "But no matter how we look, we have the same mission as everyone else—Fans First. If there's a little kid having a rough day—maybe he tried to catch a foul ball and couldn't get his hands on it—I'm going to do everything I can to get that kid a baseball and make his day."

The dad-bod guys do their best, but even they would acknowledge that we have premier dancers on our squad. I learned the importance of that when I worked with the Gastonia Grizzlies and we had our players dancing. It was still pretty new, and I was walking through the crowd when I heard a wife say to her husband, "Shut up, honey—they're about to dance!" That's when I knew we had something.

It has led to our Dancing with the Bananas competitions. The Bananas even got a nice review from the *New York Times*—not from a sportswriter, but from the newspaper's *dance* writer.

Credit for some of our best moves has to start with Maceo Harrison, our break-dancing first-base coach and the guy who teaches the choreography to our players. When fans go to a Bananas game, it's difficult for them to take their eyes off Maceo.

He's that good. Whatever dancing fans get to see on the field, that's Maceo's influence.

When we first found him, Maceo was working as a dance teacher. For a couple of years, he was Split, our mascot. Then he took over as lead dancer, where he's really invaluable. He's like a plastic man—so nimble, so flexible. Whenever the music comes on, he dances. And he's great at teaching our guys new routines, which he usually introduces to them a couple of hours before game time.

"I can break down dancing," Maceo said. "I can tell you if you need to point your toes or whatever. It's a science for me. As far as my dancing goes, I just freestyle everything. I react to whatever is going on. My head is always on a swivel. I'm always aware of what's going on around me. I play to the crowd constantly. I pick up on their energy. If they like what I'm doing, I keep it going."

Watch out, because Maceo could do a full flip at any time. We've seen him do thirty-five straight back handsprings. One time, he lined up twelve people, side by side, and flipped over the whole group. He said if he's feeling the energy, he's liable to flip right out of the stadium.

I don't think our umpire, Vincent Chapman, can flip like that. But he sure can move it. He's a high school umpire from Texarkana who was known to dance during breaks in the game, just for laughs. Well, somebody took a video and it got twelve million views on Facebook in 2013. Another one went viral in 2015. It wound up on *The Ellen DeGeneres Show*—on the Ellentube segment—and that's where we discovered him. I knew as soon as our entertainment director showed me the clip: that guy was made for Bananas games!

Vincent is stocky, sturdy, and kind of built like a fireplug. He

has a nice beard—maybe not ZZ Top quality, but considerable—
and he's known for consistency while working from behind the
plate. In short, the last thing anyone would expect from him is a
dance.

"Umpires are professional," Vincent said. "I'm calling balls and
strikes, got a great strike zone, look very professional. Then all of
a sudden, I start dancing. And people are like, 'What just happened?' Umpires aren't supposed to call attention to themselves.
I get it. But at strategic times, I'm part of the show. I love to make
people smile.

"There's a set time—the first pitch of the fourth inning—
when I'll come around to dust off the plate. Then I'll break into
a dance. That's the only thing that's planned. The rest, I pick my
spots. If I call someone out on strikes, I might make a real exag-
gerated strike-three call, then do a split. It's all part of having fun
at the ballpark. It's what the Bananas are all about."

Making it all flow is our DJ and announcer, Mark Ediss,
whom we call "Shark." Of course, he works in the Shark Tank.
He's got a playlist of a few thousand songs, along with some
movie clips, and he always seems to hit the right note. He ad-
heres to one of our basic rules: no dead air. In fact, *dead air* is a
dirty phrase around Bananaland. We always say it's somebody's
first night. He wants them walking out saying, "Wow! That was
a blast."

Our cast has something for everyone. Fans experience a wide
range of entertainment before the first pitch is even thrown.
That's our goal—to dazzle, to delight, and to have fans tell their
friends.

Fans can't help but get caught up in the fun. When fans go to
a major-league game, there are maybe three people in every section who are standing up and dancing to the music. Those people

are the weird ones, right? When fans come to a Bananas game, there are three people in every section who are *not* standing up and dancing. *They* are our weird ones.

And when the players run into the stands to celebrate with fans, it's like an all-out party has broken out.

In the theater, there's a term called the *fourth wall*. It's that invisible, imaginary wall that separates the actors from the audience. The same thing exists in sporting events. The athletes are separated from the spectators. With the Bananas, it's like that fourth wall has been torn down. Players have always seemed off-limits in professional baseball. Fans are used to looking at them like a movie. Maybe afterward, if a fan is lucky, he or she will get an autograph. But the average fan doesn't have that opportunity. When our players move through the stadium and give high fives, the fans start to realize that Bananaland is a different place.

When someone walks into our stadium, they can become one of us. Anyone can be a Banana. That's what we're all about for those three hours (which includes the pregame and postgame).

If that's not for everyone, that's OK. Look, we're not going to win the World Series, compete with the New York Yankees, or become a major-league baseball team. So why should we try to appease major-league baseball fans? We're not trying to take down MLB's $10 billion business.

We're on a mission to bring fans something they've never seen before. It's baseball, but we want to keep tweaking and twisting and changing things up. We just don't believe in maintaining the status quo forever. What's the next wave, the next fan base? What does the fan of 2025 want? What does the fan of 2030 want? What do the kids want? We're thinking about those people.

At the same time, we've realized that the players mostly like doing it differently, too. Malachi Mitchell said when he joined the Bananas, he was terrified about the fan interactions. He didn't want to mess it up. Now he loves it. He has completely bought into what we call H-3—hugs, high fives, and handshakes. He can't do them enough.

Michael Kowalski, one of our coaches, told us about taking his daughter to an Arizona Fall League game. After a hot dog, cotton candy, and a box of Sour Patch Kids, she was ready to leave. She wasn't interested in watching anything on the field. It didn't interest her in the least.

When you make the game fun—and you're obsessed with putting your fans first—the whole equation changes. The fans feel that vibe and so do the players. When a ballplayer plays freely and fearlessly—while establishing that human connection—people look forward to coming to the ballpark.

That's how we got the Bananas rolling. We entertained in a variety of ways. We listened to our fans. We made it really fun.

One day, I realized that still wasn't enough.

We had to do something more. We had to really shake up the game. And that's when Banana Ball was born.

Chapter Eleven

Changing the Game

Two seasons into our growth in Savannah—with all the singing, dancing, celebrating, fan-friendly promotions, all-inclusive prices, and accessibility to players, plus our Banana Baby, our break-dancing first-base coach, and our pep band—we were sure we were delivering the baseball product people had always wanted.

We sold out every home game. Fans had a blast. I thought it was the perfect formula.

I was wrong.

Every night, without fail, nearly half the fans gathered their stuff and just went home, usually about two hours into the game, during the fifth or sixth inning. We could have the most exciting back-and-forth baseball contest of all time or the most spectacular entertainment package ever coming between the seventh and eighth innings, but it didn't matter.

After about two hours, hundreds and hundreds of fans were done. On a weeknight, it was understandable. Their kids were restless. The adults needed rest before work in the morning. So, in the late innings our sold-out stands were more like half-full.

What could we do about that? For a century, baseball purists

had delighted in the sport's rhythm. It had no clock. It was me-
thodical, almost painfully slow at times. I mean, it was baseball.
That was how it was played, and no one could change it.

Or could they?

Once I started wondering if we could change the way the game
was played, my mind was really racing. Our motto was *Fans First.
Entertain Always*, right? Well, what did our fans really want?

I always reverted back to Henry Ford, who supposedly said,
"If you ask people what they wanted, they would have said faster
horses." Nobody was demanding an automobile. Then and now,
people don't really know what they want. Cars had to be invented
for people to realize they had such a need.

We had always listened to our fans. Now we watched them
closely. Every thirty minutes in our ballpark, usually with a cell
phone, we took videotape and pictures of the grandstands and
the seats. We took note of when people were leaving, and the
results were eye-opening.

Even with all the entertainment and the nonstop promotions—
heck, even with some folks paying ten times the face value for
tickets on the secondary market because it was the only way to get
in with all the sellouts—they were *still* leaving early, some at nine
o'clock, then even more leaving at nine fifteen and nine thirty.

I remember one of our entertainment people getting miffed
and saying, "This is just so rude, people leaving our show. You
never walk out of a movie halfway through or walk out of a Broadway show."

To me, though, it was a signal: the fans were clearly telling us
they'd had enough.

It was time for change.

It was time to invent . . . Banana Ball!

Of course, we didn't call it Banana Ball at the beginning. And we didn't exactly know the form our changes would take. But we did keep saying . . . *What if? . . . What if? . . . What if? . . .*

We viewed it like we owned a hot dog stand. Our condiments (the promotions, entertainment, and fun) were outstanding. But the hot dog itself (the baseball) still needed work. It was 2018 when we first started thinking about testing a new game. Could we deliver an experience that had never been seen before?

My dad was a big-time baseball traditionalist. He was my first confidant. We exchanged ideas about how to move the game faster and make it more fun.

I remember pacing around the kitchen at our house on Tybee Island—by then, our ball club had enjoyed some success, and we had purchased a real bed—talking to my dad on the phone, trying to figure out a way to incorporate some cool rules into the game.

"Jesse, one of the biggest issues is a blowout game," my dad said. "How can you prevent that? Fans just don't care to see that and if the score is ten to one, yeah, they're probably going to leave. These long innings are brutal. People don't want to sit through the long innings."

"But what can we do? I mean, that's baseball," I said, searching for the right words. "How can we guarantee that a game will be close and competitive without staging it?"

My dad thought for a second. He plays a lot of golf. That became his inspiration.

"What if we did it similar to golf match play?" my dad said. "Every hole counts in golf match play. What if every inning counted? What if every inning was like a chance to start over and pull even. Getting pounded in the previous inning wouldn't matter. It's a new inning, a new start. It would automatically be competitive."

I started pacing faster.

"I mean, what would that even look like in baseball?" I said.

"Well, if you win the inning one to zero or two to zero or four to two or seven to three or whatever, you get a point," my dad said. "So even though the runs were seven to three, the score is one to zero because it's only worth a point. Then you go to the next inning and you're playing for another point. It's going to automatically be a lot tighter and competitive because every inning counts."

"OK, I got it, and I think I like it . . . but how do you win the game?" I said.

"Well, if there are nine innings in a game, if you get five points, that would clinch it, right?" my dad said. "First one to five points wins."

That was our first real aha moment. Every inning *counts*. My dad got me thinking in the right direction.

Now my mind was racing.

"OK, we're going to have more competitive games, but that still doesn't solve our biggest problem," I said. "The games are going too long. People are leaving. Even if the games are great, people still leave because it's getting late. What can we do about that?"

"Somehow, you have to limit the time," my dad said. "How do you do that in baseball? I mean, baseball doesn't have a clock."

"Well, let's have a clock," I said. "Why can't we be the first baseball team with a clock?"

"So when the time runs out, the game ends right there?" my dad said.

"Something like that," I said. "If it's tied, we have to come up with a way to decide the game, something really quick and exciting. But yes, we need a clock. That way, people would actually know when the game was going to end and they could plan their night. Dad, I think this would actually be huge if we could pull it off."

"If you could limit the games to three hours, maybe two and a half, that would be great," my dad said.

"No, no, faster, faster," I said. "We have to go big here. Three hours is still too long. We watch our fans closely, Dad. We pick up on their habits. Two hours is when it starts to go bad. I think we need a two-hour clock. That's what people are really telling us that they want."

"Jesse, I think it's too much," my dad said. "People will think you're crazy. You can't change the game of baseball that much."

"Why not?" I said. "We'd have entertainment. We'd have really competitive, fun games. And we'd get people home at a reasonable hour. Perfect."

"I don't know," my dad said. "That's really fast. That's almost too fast. If you play a baseball game in two hours, people are going to want more."

I let his statement hang there a second.

"Dad, that's the idea," I said. "We want them to want more."

We were moving in the right direction. I didn't know exactly where it was going to end, but I was super excited. I started talking to our coach Tyler Gillum, and we kicked around some ideas. Tyler is super innovative and smart. He put his mind to it, and you could almost hear the gears shifting in his brain. Then I got together with Jared Orton, our team president, and we decided we should sample what other baseball leagues were doing.

Jared and I flew to Detroit to check out the United Shore Professional Baseball League games. They had four teams playing at one stadium. That seemed like a format we could use, the Savannah Bananas and three other teams playing games with our new rules. We wanted to see how people reacted. How was the attendance? What was the experience like?

We loved the stadium, but the crowd was very neutral. You

couldn't feel any passion at all. There were good aspects to it, but it wasn't exactly what we were looking for. As we talked to people and asked questions, some of them knew we were from Savannah. One guy told us, "While you're here, you've got to go to the Henry Ford Museum in Greenfield Village. You can't leave without seeing it."

So the next day, that's where we went. It was actually great. Walt Disney once went to the Henry Ford Museum, too, and found a lot of inspiration. They have a replica of the schoolhouse where Abraham Lincoln attended his classes. They have the bike shop owned by the Wright brothers—Orville and Wilbur— before they invented airplanes.

It was cool. Jared and I were walking around, taking it all in; then we noticed this little park down a hill. It looked like they were playing some sort of game. So we had to check it out.

They were playing an old-style game, a forerunner to baseball. They were dressed up in their outfits with no gloves. Some of them carried little wooden sticks. The umpire called a start to the game. The fans sat on the grass and watched. It was supposed to be 1867. I swear, it felt like we had been transported back in time.

We got whisked away, back to when things were slow and easy. Baseball was everything, even back then, but it wasn't the way it is now. This was different. Families gathered. They were all smiling, not in a hurry at all, perfectly content as they lost themselves in the game.

"Jared, I think we could do something like this," I said.

"What do you mean?" Jared said.

"We don't need to join a normal baseball league and try to fit in," I said. "We can do it ourselves. We can start a brand-new kind of game."

Jared thought about that for a minute. We kept watching the game. Could we actually take the Bananas out on their own?

"I mean, we have to think this through, but I could see where this would be the way to leave your mark," Jared said. "We'd have a chance to define the whole thing ourselves."

"Exactly," I said.

We had come to see a baseball league. We ended up going back in time, walking around a museum and seeing tributes to some of the best leaders and innovators of our time—the Wright brothers, Abraham Lincoln, and Henry Ford.

And then we happened to stumble further back in time, upon a baseball game that's different from any other baseball game? Fans were watching and enjoying themselves. What are the chances of that? This wasn't a coincidence. It couldn't have been.

Henry Ford believed in learning by doing. That was part of our inspiration, too. Jared and I looked at each other and just said, "Let's do this!"

A few months later, we played our first game with the beginnings of what we know now as Banana Ball rules.

What are the best moments in baseball? Many say walk-offs, bat flips, triples, home runs, circus catches, and plays at home plate. We asked ourselves: How do we do more of those? What are the worst moments in baseball? Let's say walks, guys constantly stepping out of the batter's box, pitchers taking forever, and the interminable games that stretch to four hours. How do we get rid of those?

Then we thought about the fans. What would be the most fans-first rule to make people really feel like they were involved in the game?

It was a ton of experimentation, innovation, and evolution—the

way we've always lived, really—to invent the structure of our Banana Ball. We essentially created nine new rules.

Two-hour time limit: The clock begins right before the first
pitch. No inning can start after the two-hour mark.

Showdown tiebreaker: If a game is tied after two hours, it goes to
a showdown, a face-off between a pitcher and a hitter. The defensive team has only a pitcher, catcher, and fielder (positioned on
the infield). If the batter is retired, the next team gets to hit. You
get just one out. If the ball is put in play, the fielder must retrieve
it (sometimes going to the outfield wall) and prevent the batter
from rounding the bases and scoring a point. The showdown continues with both teams batting until one team outscores the other.

Every inning counts: Teams get a point for scoring the most
runs in an inning. Win the inning, get the point. If the teams are
scoreless or score the same amount, that inning is even and you
go to the next one. The last inning counts the most—every run
counts as a point.

No stepping out: If a batter steps out of the box, it's a strike.

No bunting: If a batter bunts, he will be ejected.

Batters can steal first: If there's a wild pitch or passed ball at any
time, the batter can take off for first base.

No walks: On ball four, we call that a "sprint." The batter can
hustle for first base—and beyond—while the catcher quickly
throws the ball to a teammate. Each of the nine defensive players must touch the ball before the batter can be tagged out or
held on base. Fast players can wind up on third (or maybe get an
inside-the-park homer if the defense can't pull it off). It's considered an exceptional defensive effort if the throws are expeditious enough to get the runner at second.

No mound visits: Coaches, the catcher, and the other fielders are prohibited from visiting the pitcher, so there are zero need-less delays. The game keeps moving. If necessary, teammates and coaches can hype up their pitcher from afar.

And what's the way to really get fans involved in the game?

Fans can make an out: If a fan catches a foul ball on a fly, it's an out.

It wasn't exactly a linear path to get to these crazy rules.

One day when I was going for a run, I listened to this podcast about Rube Waddell, a great pitcher who played in the early twentieth century. This guy was eccentric to say the least. He had a fascination with fire trucks and would sometimes run off the field to chase them. One time, he disappeared during the off-season and they found out he was wrestling alligators in the circus. I swear, I'm not making this up.

But one of the really interesting things about Rube Waddell was how he would point to a batter and yell out, "I've got this guy." Then he would order all the defensive players off the field. It was just him and the catcher against the hitter. He would strike out the batter . . . with no defensive players! When I heard that, I almost flipped out. That was the ultimate showmanship move. That would be epic.

I looked down at my phone to note the time on the podcast, so I could go back and take notes later. I immediately thought it would be the perfect way to decide our games. It reminded me of a penalty kick in soccer, the pitcher against the hitter. Who wouldn't love that? So I was locked in on the showdown.

As soon as I wrote it down, I went to Emily and said, "I've got it! This is it! This is what we've been searching for in our game!"

Emily was washing the dishes. She kind of rolled her eyes—in a loving way, of course—then tried to humor me.

"What is it?" she said.

"It's the showdown," I said. "It's the best way to decide a game. It's like a penalty kick."

"Who's kicking?" Emily said, her face going blank.

"Kicking? What? Nobody's kicking. . . . What are you talking about?" I said, getting exasperated.

"You said it was like a penalty kick," she said.

"No, it's a showdown," I said. "Listen to me. The fans will love it. This is what we do at the end of the games. I know how we're going to do it."

"You always say, 'This is how we're going to do it,' like I should automatically understand what you're talking about," Emily said. "Jesse, not everybody thinks like you. I don't think like you. You've got to give me some context. *What* are we going to do? *Why* are we going to do it? You've got to tell people so they don't get confused."

Sometimes, I can't help myself. I get so excited. But Emily was right. Sometimes, I get over my skis and I'm going a mile a minute with my enthusiasm. People just stare at me like, *Who is that guy?* I'm not a context guy. My mind always starts at the end. In my mind, I see the perfect picture of a showdown with no one in the field and the pitcher getting a strikeout. I see the crowd going nuts. So I have to back up for people, certainly for Emily, who always asks the right questions!

But with the showdown and all the other rules we came up with, I just knew we were on the right track.

Unfortunately, we couldn't go all-in right away. As our college summer team continued to play in the Coastal Plain League, it was straight nine-inning baseball (with our added assortment of entertainment and fun, of course).

We would get there, breaking out full-scale Banana Ball for our 2021 two-game series in Mobile, Alabama, then for our seven-city World Tour regional road trip in 2022, which was highlighted by a visit to the Kansas City Monarchs, an independent league team that agreed to play us using Banana Ball rules in their ball-park.

We believe the Banana Ball rules—and we haven't given up revising them or experimenting with new concepts—will be the foundation of the Savannah Bananas as we continue to grow our fans-first movement.

But getting to this point took some work.

After the summer of 2018, after dreaming and practicing and tweaking, we needed to put the rules through a full dry-run game. I got some of my old coaches from Wofford College—one who was still there, the other who was then at Lander University—to agree to a scrimmage with their college players.

This is where it got a bit nerve-racking.

What if our new game just didn't work? What if the players couldn't adjust? What if it wasn't anything like we imagined? What then?

It was a fairly tension-filled journey to Lander University that day in my Hyundai Sonata. I was driving. Emily, Jared, and Tyler Gillum were with me, furiously going through a season's worth of statistics.

We worried about how many times a team "won" in the first five innings of regular ball. That was my biggest fear. That wouldn't be exciting at all.

"Jesse, it never happened at all," Tyler said after he checked out the final box scores of previous games.

"Oh, thank God," I said. "That's all we need, for someone to look at our new exciting rules and point out that they are actually boring."

"No chance of that," Tyler said. "It's not going to be an issue. I actually don't see a lot of times when a team will get to five points."

We were a few miles out from Lander, about to unveil our game. But we were still tinkering with the rules.

"So how does a team win?" I said. "If it's three to two, does it go to the showdown? Should every game go to the showdown?"

"Yeah, I think that would be really cool because the fans will love showdowns," Tyler said.

"Only one problem: We've never actually seen a showdown," said Jared, our voice of reason.

Emily started laughing.

"OK, let me get this straight," she said. "We're about to roll out this new game with new rules that we think will change baseball forever. And we're making up the rules as we go . . . during this car ride? Great."

"No, Emily, that's not what we're doing," I said as I punched the gas pedal. "We know exactly what we're doing."

My sarcasm wasn't lost on the crew. Then I turned to Tyler.

"Should we have just one fielder in the showdown?" I said. "Or maybe no fielders? I can't decide which would be better. I guess we've just got to see how it works."

"See?" Emily said. "Do we even know what we're doing? If we're not confident, these kids aren't going to be confident."

"Guys, we're going to be fine," Jared said. "This is going to work. We know it's going to work. We just have to do it."

"Then we better present this the right way," Emily said.

"Don't worry," I said as we pulled into the campus. "The kids are going to eat it up. I think we're going to look back on this day and remember it as a huge moment."

At least we were hoping for that. As the Lander players stood there, it looked like a lab experiment was about to begin. These guys had played hundreds of baseball games in their lives—hundreds!—but now they had the look of, *What in the world is going to happen here?*

"All right, guys, this is Jesse Cole," said Jason Burke, the Lander coach. "I want him to speak to you, so you can understand the rules again and know what you're about to do. I want you guys to have a blast. I want the same energy and intensity that we bring to every game. So, Jesse, tell these guys a little more."

This was it! The first Banana Ball game ever was about to take place. We decided to film it so we could learn from it.

I wanted to set the right tone.

"Guys, you're about to participate in the first game of what we're trying to do," I said. "The big thing we've learned in Savannah over the past three years was making a great fan experience. But what we realized is that the games also became extremely fun for the players. When the players had more fun, they played better. So it's a good experience all around for everyone.

"So today, we are intentionally experimenting. We're going to a faster, even more exciting type of game. We want more showmanship, more celebrating. So don't be afraid to let loose and have some fun. That's what this is all about. You guys good with that?"

They looked around, then started nodding and smiling. The players were open to our ideas. When we first explained the rules, they laughed at some of them.

"What do you mean . . . we can steal first? And if we step out, it's a strike?"

They cackled like schoolkids. This was all so new.

So away we went.

I'll never forget what happened in the fourth inning. A new pitcher came to the mound—and everyone stopped. There were maybe ten girlfriends of the players in the stands because the game was essentially a practice. They were doing homework. But when the pitcher came in to start a new at bat, all the girlfriends stopped and started watching the game.

This guy was throwing a pitch every six to seven seconds. Everyone in the stands was murmuring, wondering what was happening. The pitcher would get the ball back and throw again immediately. The entire at bat took under a minute. It was unreal.

Forty minutes into the game, we were in the sixth inning. They were all like, *What?*

We wanted the pitchers to work as fast as they could, but one particular pitcher (a Banana-in-waiting?) took it to another level. We had somebody throw three pitches in about twelve seconds for a strikeout. It was so mind-blowing for people accustomed to baseball's normal pace. We played a full nine innings in ninety-nine minutes.

Afterward, all the players were smiling. They were like, "That was so much fun. It was so fast and awesome. We were constantly on our toes. There was no downtime."

And that's exactly what we wanted.

"Guys, the Bananas want some feedback," the Lander manager said. "Ask any question you want. Basically, they want to know what you liked and what you disliked. What needs to change? Again, they're not looking to change baseball. They want to make baseball appealing to more people. For people who don't like our game because it's too slow or there's not enough action, they want to add a faster-paced game and showmanship. They're trying to get more people to like the game that you guys have always loved. Any feedback you give is huge."

I added this: "Guys, did it feel like every inning was made more important? Did it seem like a normal and natural game?"

Again, the players all smiled, looked around, and nodded.

"We had a blast!"

"It was great having it move so fast."

"That's the way the game seemed when I was a kid."

"Once you got used to it, it was great."

As we walked off the field, one player lingered and tried to get my attention.

"I think you guys have got a good future with this," he said.

Sweet music to my ears!

As we continued to test the rules with our players and get the game ready for full-scale use, the pace of play became the most popular aspect. Seeing two hours of fast-paced baseball—and feeling like you've seen a complete game and missed no moments of consequence—became the foundation of our fans-first approach. Even if we've only reached the sixth inning by our time limit, taking into consideration the constant entertainment and no dead time, that's still a full night. Plus, unlike at a conventional baseball game, spectators can stay until the end and still get home at a reasonable time.

Mary Carillo came to Savannah in 2022 to do a feature on us for HBO's *Real Sports*. She had only vaguely heard of the Savannah Bananas and wasn't familiar with how we played the game. Well, she got up to speed quickly. And she absolutely loved the notion of completing a baseball game in a predictable two-hour window.

Mary had also played professional tennis, and tennis tournaments made up the bulk of her work when she began her broadcasting career. Tennis has a similar problem. In Grand Slam events, a men's match could go three sets or five sets. It could be done in a couple of hours . . . or it could linger for four or five hours.

"Look, except for sleep, there's nothing I want to do for more than two hours at a time," Mary said. "I mean, nothing. Maybe that's a function of age. But whether it's a meal, a movie, a party, a date, a game . . . two hours and I'm out. There's nothing to stop that.

"I've done plenty of bad four-hour tennis matches. The interest level is over so much earlier than the actual match. This Banana Ball thing is pretty genius. Two and out. Kids can come. Older people can come. You know what time you're getting home. And there's such constant joy and passion throughout the stadium. It's like British soccer without the drunkenness."

During the COVID summer of 2020, before the major leagues came back for their shortened season, the Bananas were one of the few baseball teams in action. We played a revised schedule because nearly all the other league teams were inactive, so we were able to use Banana Ball rules. We played a full nine-inning intersquad Banana Ball game, and it took only one hour and forty-eight minutes.

From a practical standpoint—for a fan or a television programmer—that's ideal. As overscheduled as people are these days, it's comforting for fans to know when the game's end point could be reached. NFL and college football games can bleed into the three-and-a-half- or four-hour marks these days, but those are only once a week. If there were 162 NFL games—a baseball-style calendar—would people watch all of those?

Players love the compacted, predictable schedule as well.

"I think this is what players prefer," said Jake Skole, a former first-round pick who played on our 2022 World Tour team. "In other baseball, you have guys constantly complaining with umpires. You have guys who are trained by their mental coaches to slow things down and focus, but that pace does not energize the fan base. With Banana Ball, you don't have time for anything other than playing fast and playing hard. You better put your ego aside and focus or else you're looking at strike two. This game moves fast."

Nothing moves faster than our "sprint," which is what the batter does after drawing ball four. At first, it was disastrous. The catcher didn't know where to throw and the batter had a great chance of getting around the bases. Now it has been refined and it's a race. It's way more competitive and exciting than a walk, which was pretty darn boring.

The showdown tiebreaker has exciting elements, too. It's like kids on a playground. The defensive player might have to run to the outfield wall and see if he can throw the ball in before the batter races home. It gets the blood pumping, and it's a fantastic way to decide a game. At first, some people wanted us to settle games with a home run derby. No. That's *wayyyy* too slow. The showdown pulls spectators out of their stadium seats.

"The showdown is mano a mano . . . who's going to beat who?" said Dakota McFadden, one of our top two-way players. "He wants to get you. You want to get him. Don't you think that would sell or be great television?

"All the Banana Ball rules promote throwing strikes and putting the ball in play. That eliminates the deadwood, the boring parts of the game that put people to sleep. That's why our fans are so into it. There's always something cool going on."

Of course, all the fans are completely fascinated by the prospect of catching a foul ball to make an out. It happened half a dozen times on our 2022 World Tour, and it almost happened three times in one game. We usually bring the fan down to our dugout for some props. It's pretty cool for anyone to catch a foul ball—period—but the idea of helping the Bananas get out of an inning? Over the top! Of course, if a Banana batter hits a foul ball, we politely ask for fans to allow the ball to drop. The surrounding fans are pretty good about enforcing that.

All the twists, tweaks, and rule adjustments are designed to make the game more fun, faster-moving, and more appealing, especially for those who aren't avidly into baseball. Adam Virant, one of our coaches, uses the climate change analogy and suggests thinking of baseball as a glacier: it's moving slowly, but subtly ripping apart. One day, as kids continue to develop shorter attention spans, will the new generation even bother to watch if baseball hasn't adapted its pace?

When we did the two nights in Mobile, Alabama, before our summer Coastal Plain season of 2021, Banana Ball rules got its biggest showcase of all. Mobile had lost its Double A minor-league team, and we sold out both games pretty quickly. We called it a One-City Word Tour and it was the first tangible proof that Banana Ball would work well outside of Savannah. We added some players to form the Party Animals, who would be the Bananas' opponent.

We worked closely with Jake Peavy, the former MLB pitcher who won the National League Cy Young Award in 2007 and played in three All-Star Games. He's a Mobile native who really cares about his hometown. After the minor-league team departed, Jake helped to attract other events into their stadium, and that was his introduction to the Bananas.

Jake, who also works for the MLB Network, is one of our biggest advocates.

"I want to be the connective tissue to Major League Baseball and the Savannah Bananas," Jake said. "I wouldn't in any way do that if I didn't believe and respect Jesse and his vision. I'm such a sucker for any dreamer. I'm the same dude.

"It's undeniable that fans are wanting and enjoying what the Bananas are providing. These Banana Ball rules are brilliant. I think with analytics and shifts and these other things, some of baseball's soul has been stripped away. The Bananas are bringing back the human element, the kind of baseball we all remember when we were kids, when it was so fun. That's Banana Ball in a word—fun."

Jake said he had become jaded by baseball after his exit from the game. He couldn't imagine such negative emotions with the Bananas. To his sons and younger buddies who took in the Mobile games, the Savannah Bananas might as well have been the Boston Red Sox. With our entertaining style and our players' availability for autographs, a huge impression was made.

"Banana Ball is a completely different experience than I ever imagined having around baseball," Jake said. "Let's be real, man. We have such a short time on earth. And I mean, we have tons of serious moments in there. Coming to a ballpark should be in the name of fun, fellowship, enjoying each other's company, eating hot dogs, and watching the players compete.

"Banana Ball encapsulates that. Since my boys had that experience, they haven't worn another team hat."

I know exactly what Jake is talking about. Baseball means family.

Chapter Twelve

Family

My earliest memories of baseball are of playing catch with my father. Now I am absolutely thrilled to have my father still involved, whether it's through talking to him on a daily basis, having him help craft the ideas for Banana Ball rules, or being someone I can look to in the stands for assurance.

Banana Ball also means family. As Emily and I build this business—and hopefully bring a whole new enthusiasm to baseball—our kids are growing up at the ballpark. We're building great memories.

That's right, our kids.

For a long time, Emily and I weren't sure how we wanted to grow our family. I was an only child. I was fine with having one kid and stopping. Emily had three siblings, and, as she put it, she "knew what it was like to have three best friends in the house with me."

Emily painted the picture of our future. She wanted the big Thanksgiving table with all the kids coming home from college together. If we had just one kid, what if they didn't want to get married? We did a lot of talking and debating. After thinking about it, I came around. I liked the idea of a house full of kids.

Emily cares so much about people, and I think I have a big heart, too. When we had considered all of those factors, it led to us becoming foster parents. I can't say it was something I'd had in mind—ever—but the more we thought about it, the more sense it made for us.

By the time Banana Ball hit its stride in 2022, we had three children who were age four or younger—a full house. As crazy as our life gets sometimes, we wouldn't have it any other way.

Our biological son, Maverick, was born in 2018, and just after his second birthday, we became foster parents for Kenna, who was three months younger. In 2021, we agreed to foster Addison; she arrived when she was six days old. That gave us three kids in the house.

Foster parenting isn't for everyone. We understand that. But after Emily did her research and told me there were more than 500,000 kids in the United States who don't have a permanent home, that was a pivotal day for me. There are about 214,000 licensed foster homes and that figure has slightly declined over the last five years. We felt like we had to help and that we should do it. Our thought process was along the lines of "whatever happens in the future, we'll find a way to figure it out."

Emily and I try to see things for what they could be. Many kids in care, and ours are no exception, get off to a rough start in life, but we believe in their potential. We nurture the positives. We tend to see things for what they could be instead of what they are now. Every person has potential.

Emily messages more people than I could ever imagine. If someone needs their spirit lifted, she will listen and provide encouragement. Emily cares deeply about people and quietly supports charities that are dear to her heart. In baseball terms, it's like when you see how someone practices or plays when they think no one is watching. That shows character. Emily does heroic things every day and she took the lead on how we built our family.

Even when she was ready to deliver our son, Maverick, she had a difficult time, but she still had the presence of mind to make sure I was all right. She was in the hospital room and all these machines started beeping, louder and louder. Suddenly, the doctor who was going to deliver Maverick started frantically calling people.

The next thing I knew, there were nine nurses there. The doctor was telling them to move left, move right. Now they were saying, "Priority one!" I didn't even know what that meant. We were going to emergency surgery. The baby's heart rate was about forty. And as Emily was getting wheeled off, she turned to one of the nurses, pointed at me, and said, "Take care of him. Make sure he's OK." They had to get her in there and deliver Maverick within five minutes. It was so scary. And one of Emily's priorities was making sure I was OK.

We had plenty on our plate with a newborn, but throughout the pregnancy, Emily looked ahead. She started researching foster care and found that there were half a million kids already born who are in the foster care system, according to the federal Adoption and Foster Care Analysis and Reporting System.

Emily dug pretty deep with reading and listened to podcasts for months. The more she learned, the more intriguing it became. It started weighing on her mind constantly. We went for walks with Maverick, who was now eighteen months old, and we talked more seriously about becoming foster parents.

A common pitfall among couples is one partner being on board with foster care and the other not quite being there. And they tell prospective foster parents that if both partners are not 100 percent on board—with so much trauma and so many issues and challenges involved in the process—it could break up their relationship very easily.

I had hundreds of questions. Emily knew every day that I was scared of the foster care process, mostly because of selfish reasons. A litany of questions ran through my mind: *How would it affect our family? Would this affect Maverick? What would it do to us? What about our time together? I love what we're doing with the Bananas; how will all of that work now?*

But the more I heard the stories Emily was telling me, the more I listened to podcasts, I knew the lack of foster families was a bigger problem than I ever would have guessed. It just isn't emphasized much or talked about in our society.

All along, we thought our home base was going to be the Charlotte, North Carolina, area, with Gastonia nearby. When the Savannah opportunity came about, we moved to Georgia. It was a tough thing for Emily at first because her family, her friends, and a really good support system were in Charlotte.

Our research of the foster care system indicated foster parents needed a strong support system because the whole thing could fall apart if there wasn't a network in place. So to do this, we had to commit to living in two places. We received our foster care license in North Carolina, and it was finalized in December of 2020. At least for a while, we were not going to be in Savannah all the time.

But it gave Jared Orton, our president, an opportunity to probably grow and take the reins of our Bananas organization. I still struggled with our potential situation and asked Emily, "Do you know anybody who has a job five hours away and is running the kind of business that we are? I'd like to find them and talk to them."

Emily thought about it and said, "How often do you look to copy somebody? We figure things out. We find ways to do things better. We always see the potential in things."

Of course, Emily was right.

The whole process carried such uncertainty. When families foster a child, it could be for two months. It could be for a year, or even longer. We started the process on Maverick's birthday, May 4, 2020. Emily got a call in January 2021, and we were asked to pick up a child that day. That's how fast it works. Kenna was two at the time.

Initially, she was placed in a home with her brothers and a foster family. Two days later, the foster family said they couldn't keep all three. It was too much. Agencies try to keep the siblings together, but sometimes they can't, so in this case she came to live with us.

In the weeks before that, we had told Maverick that we might have a friend come stay with us. He was only two and a half years old. We said, "They don't have any toys or clothes or food. Can you share?" Maverick nodded, so he knew he was going to share with somebody.

Emily had learned about this—telling your kids about the potential arrival of a foster child—as she dug into all the information. She was obsessed with learning as much as possible. She also saw a bigger picture. She knew the Bananas were growing and a lot of people were starting to look up to us. We could be advocates for foster parenting.

The first day seemed to go well. Kenna played with Maverick. Had it just been Emily and me, maybe it would've been awkward. Kids attach to kids. The night didn't go too well at all. Certain things triggered her fears, and she did not want to be in the dark. So I sat in a chair all night and held her as she fell asleep on my chest.

The first couple of weeks were tough. We tried to help her adjust, just getting her to sleep on our laps while we held her in her room. Then we got her to sleep on the floor with a crib next to us. Then she slept in the crib while I was just outside of it holding her hand. We had to progress very slowly.

It took a few months, but it finally got smoother. She started asking to take naps. She asked for veggies and fruits with her meals.

As hard as it was, we quickly gained an appreciation for the importance of foster parenting and how much it was needed. We now have a dream of starting a nonprofit to help the foster care world. As we travel and go to different cities, we hope to make a local impact by raising awareness of the need for foster families. We would get the foster families to attend our games and recognize them in a special way. We would also raise money by donating a portion of all the money taken in during the game.

The name of our nonprofit will be, well, Bananas Foster.

When I told Emily my idea for the name, she got emotional. She just nodded.

Now that we were in the groove with two toddlers, our home was open for other children if we got "the call." But we were in Savannah for the summer of 2021, so we put the process on hold until we could get back to North Carolina, where we were licensed. In October, the foster care agency called and asked if we were still able to take in more kids. We said yes.

Two weeks later, Emily and I were heading out on a date night when the cell phone rang. It was the foster agency calling to tell us that a six-day-old baby girl needed a home starting that night. If we could provide care for her, we needed to come in right then to the hospital for a few hours of training. The health and medical issues we would face with Addison were able to be overcome, but it was going to be a rough road for a while. And rough it was! But all these experiences just added to the strength of our relationship.

For six days, Addison went through the worst of it in the NICU. She detoxed for a few more weeks at home. It was difficult to change her diaper because her body was so stiff. Addison was fighting drugs in her tiny little system.

Neither Emily nor I would have become a foster parent on our own. But we are in this together and our support system is amazing.

No logical people would have done all that we're doing at one time. On paper, we had a business that was growing like crazy. We were primarily living five hours away. We already had one child, then another one. And now we were bringing in a baby?

Whatever comes our way at this point doesn't scare us because we know we can handle it. We read a book together by Marie Forleo titled *Everything Is Figureoutable*, and we sort of live by that mantra now. Yes, we could be going through a lot, but it's likely just a season. You can have challenging seasons, but they don't last forever. And the eternal optimist in me thinks something great will come out of the tough times. We have learned so much, including the best ways to make our marriage even stronger.

I think one mistake some couples make is pouring all their energy into their children and not spending enough energy on each other. One day, they might discover they don't have much in common and wonder what happened to the relationship that had been so good when they got married.

Emily and I are not going to allow that to happen. We love our kids, but a strong marriage and partnership is our top priority.

We carry this over to the Bananas as well. We want to make sure our people recharge and take the time they need. The organization is growing quickly. Emily and I can work our butts off. But none of that matters if we don't take care of our people. They are on the front line. When we're on tour, we want to balance our work with culture and fun outings because that helps our people feel loved and appreciated.

That's how a family works, too.

Chapter Thirteen

The Tryout

It was a beautiful sixty-five-degree Saturday morning in 2022, not what most people expect in late February, but in perfect character for Savannah. Not long after sunrise, just as our staff had gulped down their coffees and braced themselves for one of the most thrilling days in Bananas history, a procession of players arrived at Grayson Stadium.

These were young, chiseled athletes. Some had that tough-guy look. They carried bat bags, gloves, and spikes. Your standard baseball tryout, right? Yeah, not exactly.

One guy was dressed like a hot dog.

Another resembled a fairy princess.

There's nothing like being jolted awake by the sight of a man wearing an XXL shirt and an extra-snug ballerina tutu. There's nothing more cool than a locked-in outfielder with smeared eye black wearing an elf's outfit. And to completely steal my heart, there was the guy in full flannel banana gear.

As everyone assembled in the stands, I was practically bursting with pride. This was one heck of a crew! There was a World Series pitcher, a Major League Baseball All-Star, a former first-round draft pick, and a few dozen guys with professional baseball experience.

There were also a tap dancer, a juggler, a merengue dancer, a professional bronc rider, an insect exterminator, a professional bodybuilder, a guy who imitated funny animal noises, a police officer, an Amazon delivery-truck driver, a singer/songwriter, a rodeo clown, a firefighter, some former mascots, a gymnast, a black belt in karate, a guy who described himself as a cat trainer, and the first baseball athlete to ever play on stilts.

We didn't ask them for an unusual skill or talent. We didn't suggest that they wear something outlandishly eye-catching. We demanded it.

"Today, we are trying to create the greatest show in sports, and we are looking for the greatest showmen," I told them. "This is your opportunity to play baseball in a different way and have the time of your life."

"LET'S GO!" somebody yelled from the crowd.

I couldn't agree more. Let's go!

There were seventy-plus participants. Only about half would make our Banana Ball premier teams for the seven-city World Tour. Some would become Bananas. The others would be Party Animals, the tour's antiheroes. We could divide the teams later. First, there was work to do.

We needed a mix of baseball players, entertainers, and guys who dazzled spectators with their talents and tricks. If a player hesitated while expressing himself or wasn't all-in on the fun— no disrespect—the Bananas probably weren't the right fit.

This wasn't just a baseball tryout.

We flat-out wanted it to be the greatest tryout ever.

I think it was. It set in motion an incredible ninety days for the Bananas, where we played to continuous sellout crowds, got more attention than ever, and showed the world that Banana Ball was here to stay. So how did we get to this pivotal moment of evaluating talent and picking our teams in one crazy, exhausting, and often hilarious day?

Let's back up a few months.

When we sold out Mobile in 2021, it became clear that we needed to keep growing. Savannah had been our home base— our city on the hill—but the world was our stage. We needed to take this Banana show on the road with an expanded World Tour. To do that, we needed more players, so we could have enough pitching for two teams and potential back-to-back games. We needed more crazy talents than ever before. But before that, we needed a head coach.

That's right, a head coach. Language is very important, and I know baseball purists are probably saying, "Jesse, you idiot. Football has head coaches. Baseball has managers."

Well, we're a little different in Bananaland.

We believe that people want to be led. They don't want to be managed. So, we have no managers on our staff—or general managers, for that matter. It might seem like a tiny thing, but that's our mindset. The big leaguers have managers. They might call him Skipper or Skip as part of the time-honored protocol. Banana Ball has leaders. If there must be a title, it's coach.

So who could we get to coach the greatest show in sports?

We kept coming back to Eric Byrnes, a former major leaguer, a live wire if there ever was one, a bundle of energy and outrageousness, a guy who never took himself too seriously, a huge personality, a guy who knew only one way to live—full-throttle.

He sounded like a ripe Banana to me.

Whenever I scrolled through social media, I'd come across Byrnes doing something crazy. There would always be a comment from someone saying something like, "Man, he would be the perfect Savannah Banana." The more I thought about it, the more it made sense.

Byrnesie had name recognition and credibility. He'd played eleven seasons in the big leagues, mostly with the Oakland A's and Arizona Diamondbacks. He'd had a season with twenty homers and fifty stolen bases—only ten other guys *ever* have done that. He was an analyst for the MLB Network. But more than all of that, he brought so much electricity and energy when he played the game.

So we contacted him and set up a call. He showed interest but also had a ton of questions. What about our vision? What about our roster? What about our yellow pants?

Here's the really cool part, the thing that illustrates why the Bananas are the future. At first, Byrnesie said he was aware of the Bananas in a kinda, sorta way. But his eleven-year-old son swayed the conversation and said, "Dad, you've got to talk to them. The Bananas are the best!" Once we started describing our big vision to Byrnesie and explained to him about our goal to make baseball fun again, I think he was in.

We didn't offer him anything immediately. We made a few more calls. But we moved fast. In typical Bananas style, we didn't have an ordinary job interview. Byrnesie had zero coaching experience other than his son's baseball team, but I talked to Berry Aldridge, our baseball operations coordinator, and we agreed that this was our guy. It was pure Bananas logic. The guy who would coach our professional team? Of course his only coaching experience would have been with a team of eleven-year-olds. That was perfect.

On the first call, Byrnesie asked if I had seen any of his videos with the eleven-year-old team. Um, no, not really, so I checked them out. In the videos, he's shown sprinting down the third-base line as the runner is coming home. He looks like he goes crazy as he celebrates with his team.

Between that on-field juice and the respect I knew he would command from having played in the majors, it looked like a great fit. Plus, Byrnesie is an absolute maniac. He did a triathlon across the entire country—swimming 7 miles, cycling 2,350 miles, and running 850 miles to go from San Francisco to New York. Just crazy. He has also played one hundred and twenty holes of golf in a day, running 109 miles while breaking the Guinness record. He knew his baseball, but he was also up for anything.

I knew he could bring energy and excitement. Sure, I still had some question marks. The major leagues and Banana Ball are two different things. But we were all-in, and then when we brought Byrnesie to Savannah for his introductory news conference, he did a video interview with Biko Skalla, our broadcast entertainer.

Both Byrnesie and Biko were in a bathtub when the interview was conducted.

Let's call that a Banana baptism. Byrnesie was officially one of us.

For more than two months leading up to the tryout, we had audio or video calls every Wednesday. The calls would consist of Berry and me, plus our two full-time players, Bill LeRoy and Kyle Luigs, along with Byrnesie and the coaches, Mike Kowalski, Adam "Mo" Moreau, and Adam Virant, whom we know as Viro. Viro is the coach of the Party Animals. Sometimes our entertainment and social media staff would be on the call, too.

Teams normally do not have eight to ten weekly calls with eight to ten people when planning a normal baseball tryout. But remember, we were planning the greatest tryout ever.

I wanted the tryout to be bigger and better than any that these players had ever been to or could even imagine. This was these players' first exposure to our vision, and they needed to have an experience dramatically different from anything else they had been part of on a baseball field.

I wanted energy, speed, passion, and fun. And for the guys who didn't make our team, I wanted them to say that it had been the most fun tryout ever. I believe every time we interact with someone, especially players, we have an opportunity to create a potential fan who believes in Banana Ball and hopefully tells a friend.

We sent a video to all the players we selected for the tryout and told them not to dress like everybody else. This was different from our college team, where we got players from different schools, then trained them in dancing and other stunts. From the start, we wanted our tryout players to be showmen and to stand out and amplify their talents. That set the tone. We weren't looking for typical baseball players. We also mentioned/told them that if they weren't the kind of person or player who would be willing to be a showman, it wasn't the tryout for them.

In the future, our tryouts may be something we document for social media content, but not the place where we pick our entire team. We have a strong nucleus and solid referrals, so selecting an entire team from scratch won't be necessary. It will be more like an open tryout in the major leagues, where two hundred guys show up and they might keep one or two.

But at this first tryout, we had a lot of moving parts. How could we get the right players who performed at a high level, while also being showmen? What would the actual format of the tryout be? How would we evaluate these guys? How much fun could they possibly have? If we tested them with dances, TikTok videos, celebrations, diving plays, and trick plays, how would they respond?

We decided to evaluate the players with a series of baseball-related drills, along with entertainment displays that would bring out their personalities. We needed to see all sides of each player. I thought the tryout format worked beautifully. Give the credit to Viro, who really planned it out.

Viro is a smart guy. He played ball in junior college and at George Mason University and then went to law school to become a sports agent. As it turned out, he spent a lot of money to learn that he hated being a lawyer. One of his buddies was coaching with the Bananas and turned Viro back on to baseball. Viro said that decision probably saved his life. And he's been great for us, too.

The night before the tryout, our contingent of ten people—coaches and entertainment staff—gathered on the right-field party deck at Grayson. I had my game face on because it was going to be crucial that we select the right mix of players. The rush-hour crowd was headed down Victory Drive, which encompasses the park, and a few joggers circled the park outside the stadium. The sun was going down, and it had started to cool off, so it was long-sleeve weather.

If anyone saw us standing around the large high-top tables on the party deck, it probably looked like a bunch of guys about to pop some cold ones at Friday's happy hour. I don't think any of us felt that relaxed. This was like the most intense round of speed-dating one could imagine. It was a crash course. We didn't have much time, and we had to find our team.

Byrnesie and Kowalski, who had traveled from the West Coast, joined us, arriving from the airport together, wearing matching Bananas blazers and carrying canary yellow roller suitcases, and we got down to business.

Where to start? We had made magnetized baseball cards that

contained photos and information for each player. We arranged them on two whiteboards, assembling them into the different categories:

No Doubters: The ones we hope will be with us, no matter what.
Must Watch: They are close to being Bananas. They probably just need to perform.
Must Wow: To make our team, they have to do something unbelievable.
Entertainers: The guys with special talents.

We knew some of these guys well from past Bananas experience. Some of those players had brought along teammates they recommended from their independent league stops, so those guys had ready-made credibility.

Some players we didn't know at all, and that was a problem. The way the tryout was set up—with ninety players doing so many things in just one day and us making roster decisions almost immediately—we figured we would make some mistakes. As it turned out, with the exception of a player or two, I think we did unbelievably great under those expeditious conditions.

Viro's organization made that happen. We wrapped up our evening meeting by eight o'clock, when it began to get dark, grabbed some quick sleep, and were all back at the ballpark by 7:00 a.m., ninety minutes before we started checking in the players.

Viro labeled the different parts of the tryout as "acts." Act I was the welcome. Act II was the preshow, the warm-up. Act III was showtime, the entertainment interviews for pitchers and the drills for position players. Act IV was Banana Ball, the game itself. Act V was the announcement. Even with the incredible number of players we needed to watch in a short time—there were thirty-five pitchers alone—it all ran on schedule.

This wasn't exactly a closed tryout. ESPN was there documenting every move. We were filming for our social media channels. The media was invited.

We started teaching our players the weave as they shuffled along the infield, passing the baseball from player to player, Harlem Globetrotters–style. It was too slow and too cumbersome. We didn't have the time to make that work. So we quickly moved to teaching them how to sing and dance to "Hey Baby," a real staple of our fan participation. Nearly every player jumped around happily throughout the act; their lively animation made me smile.

When the position players started their drills, the pitchers went into interviews with Biko in the clubhouse. That's where some newcomers really got pushed out of their comfort zone. Biko offered choices. They could wrestle him as the interview took place. They could do an interpretive dance. They could wear headphones and turn the music up loud, giving answers to questions they couldn't hear. Or they could interview themselves.

Some guys were hilarious. Others kind of shrugged and said they'd give it a try. In both cases, we learned more about their personalities and how they would play as Bananas.

I loved the position drills, especially with the outfielders. They took turns at launching throws to the backstop, aiming at third-base targets, catching easy fly balls with flair and robbing home run balls over the wall.

Once we got into Banana Ball, it was way too much of a grind, mostly because so many pitchers needed to work. We were about twenty pitchers in during the day, and things started dragging. That's when we had Zack Frongillo, our director of entertainment, mix in a changeup.

On command, he asked the participants for an impromptu round of "Hey Baby."

As I looked around, every player was singing, dancing, and smiling, whether they were in the infield, the outfield, or the bullpen. It was cool.

Something else really cool was how quickly Byrnesie adjusted to what we wanted in a Bananas player. He pushed more for the entertainment than I did. I'd never had that in a coach—ever. I'd always had to push and push and push. With Byrnesie, I had to tone him down.

Surrounded by the on-field chaos, Byrnesie did a TV interview. In the background of the shot, a guy wearing a Tony the Tiger outfit played catch with a guy wearing rodeo chaps. Without missing a beat, Byrnesie told the interviewer: "Look at that. There's a guy in the batting cage wearing Daisy Dukes. Hey, he's got a pretty good swing!"

Just another day in Bananaland.

When it came to evaluations, Byrnesie and I didn't see eye to eye on everything. We're both type A personalities and not looking to defer. I was skeptical about one player, but Byrnesie told me, "Jesse, he's doing backflips. He's a Savannah Banana." He was taken with guys who were unbelievably athletic and thought the rest could be figured out.

Bottom line: He was all-in with making it a better show experience, which was perfect for a Bananas coach. And I think we both learned a lot from each other, as we worked to make everything balance.

Of course we all would've loved more time to deliberate. As Viro put it, we really needed "some moments of sober reflection." But we were under the gun. Just like every sports team, we made some decisions people could second-guess.

We didn't initially keep Christopher Vazquez, a professional player with Bananas experience. He didn't have a great tryout. That one hurt the most for me. He didn't show well. Byrnesie and Kowalski didn't know him. In baseball, a player can be over-exposed in one day, but if the coaching staff sees a guy every day over time, they get a better feel.

We kept Chad Beaver, a shortstop, mostly because he was great at doing backflips. But we already had other guys doing the backflips, so maybe that was overvalued. William Kwasigroh wore a sombrero and made a spectacular diving catch in left field. It was awesome. We couldn't get enough of that. But he wasn't a position player; he was a pitcher.

I think we mostly got it right, but our future tryouts will be even more structured and focused. I see us with more people in the stands as evaluators. I think we will put more artificial pressure on the pitchers, maybe giving them two minutes to throw as many strikes as possible. In Banana Ball, teams (or pitchers) lose more games with walks than by the other team getting hits.

Nearly every guy out there told us it had been the most enjoyable tryout they had seen and they'd had fun. Our tryout was so popular that Bill Lee—"the Spaceman" himself—showed up and made our team. I had a fear about what this seventy-five-year-old man, this Boston Red Sox Hall of Fame pitcher, was really thinking. I mean, guys were dressed in costumes and there was dancing practice. It was like a circus. He might have seen this and turned around.

But Bill Lee was dubbed "the Spaceman" for good reason. During his major-league career, he was eccentric, irreverent, outrageous, and highly quotable. Many of his comments were tongue-in-cheek and over the heads of his audience. He probably is best known for his eephus pitch, a slow, high-arching rainbow lob that baffled batters, who were accustomed to a fast pace. Bill, ever the controversial counterculture figure, was highly critical of baseball's establishment and claimed he was "blackballed" after being released by the Montreal Expos in 1982.

Bill vowed to keep playing baseball, and that's what he did—in a variety of semiprofessional leagues—and he worked as a celebrity pitcher at many events.

Bill Lee and the Savannah Bananas seemed like a marriage made in baseball entertainment heaven. We had contacted him about the tryout, and he definitely seemed interested. At the end of the tryout, Bill said he had never seen guys having more fun while playing ball together. When he realized what Banana Ball was, even Bill Lee had to be a Banana.

When we were finally done on tryout day, I think Byrnesie was a little stunned. There was so much to process. He said to the players, "I don't know what I just witnessed, but it was glorious."

After making our decisions, someone said we should read off the roster like it was *The Price Is Right*. As in . . . "Come on down!" Or perhaps make it like a beauty pageant, where the players would be lined up and the winners would be announced, perhaps even being crowned.

None of that fit. So we went into the stands to read off the names and congratulate the players and thank the ones who didn't make it. There was work ahead—separating the players into the Bananas and the Party Animals, the opposing team that served as the scruffy-looking villains. But that could wait.

I wanted to savor the moment. We were making baseball history—and we'd had so much fun. Now it was time to buckle up. We were about to begin one hell of a ride. "As much of a crazy show that this is, we've got a job to do," Byrnesie told our guys. "And that job is to positively influence an entire new generation of baseball fans while we show them what's possible."

I couldn't agree more, Byrnesie!

LET'S GOOOOOO!

Chapter Fourteen

Social Media

I t's crazy to think about this now, but in the summer of 2020, I'm not sure I could have told you much about TikTok. What was it? A clock? No, I was told. It was "sort of a dance app." Something the cool kids watched on their phones.

Oh, how times have changed. The Savannah Bananas have been described in media reports as "TikTok's Favorite Team" and I think I understand the app and its potential about as well as anyone in the world of sports.

It's true. The Bananas are all about TikTok, those short bursts of music, dancing, craziness, and fun. If you want to know the truth, we live in a TikTok world. A lot of kids don't read books unless they have a school assignment, but they watch videos. Specifically, they like quick videos. With so much competition for America's shrinking attention span, those seeking a TikTok following need to stand out.

And that's why the Savannah Bananas are perfect for social media—specifically TikTok. When we hit three million TikTok followers—a figure that still stuns me—it was more than triple the number for the highest Major League Baseball team.

More than triple!

We made the decision a long time ago that traditional marketing could take us only so far. *For sale! Buy now!* Blah, blah, blah. Give the fans some credit. They already know we have a service. They already know we have games. They already know we offer merchandise.

Beyond all of that obvious stuff, we wanted to be the coolest brand possible. We wanted to provide media content our fans would love and enjoy, whether it was videos, a docuseries, or outrageous dance video clips. If they wanted to buy something, that would have been awesome, but we weren't going to shove merchandise down their throats.

We're just a bunch of folks who want to make baseball fun. Our team comes up with great ideas, no question. But the ideas themselves aren't what makes it special. It's our *willingness* to do it. It's our process of weighing the options, imagining the response, and being a little more crazy than people might expect.

Our live show is the first barometer of what works and what doesn't. How do people react? If I hear them cheering, that's good. I watch what happens at each moment and think about what comes next. And I listen. I always listen for reactions. If the current thing doesn't work, will the next thing?

Then we share our fun on social media. We mostly focus on an audience that doesn't like baseball. Most teams try to appease their season ticket holders, which is a very small minority of those in attendance. The Bananas try to attract and appease a much larger base. That could include a lot of five-year-olds, nine-year-olds, and ninety-year-olds.

When we started our 2022 World Tour in Daytona Beach, we had about four thousand people in the stadium, which was great. But our social media videos were viewed twenty-five million times that week. When we have a game that we broadcast live on social media, there's also a much bigger picture that's taking place, which we can measure. Between the reaction of our in-person crowd and the size of our social media presence, we get a great indication about what's working and what isn't.

In the week between our tour stops at Daytona Beach and West Palm Beach, we added more than 100,000 followers to Tik-Tok. That's because we delivered a great show at Daytona and videoed the best moments. That's how we build momentum. We put on an entertaining event and get tremendous word-of-mouth recommendations. When fans view our videos and like them, it usually drives them to attend or view the next event. When we play, it's like a live Broadway performance. We hear the cheers. We slap high fives. We take our bows. We are creating new fans, not only at the game site, but all over the world.

That is the power of social media.

That is why TikTok matters so much to us.

I think we were behind on Facebook, Twitter, Instagram, and the other platforms because we were still trying to figure out how to best utilize them. When the TikTok platform came into popularity, the frenetic pace and youthful audience fit perfectly for what we had been preaching. We created Banana Ball to speed up the pace of slow and boring baseball games. Then two years into our "faster, faster, faster" theme, we found a perfect social media match in TikTok.

Some people think everything the Bananas do is scripted to create viral moments on TikTok. Although we love those viral moments, the foundation of what we do is to create things people have never seen on a baseball field.

We love when our players do choreographed dances, then throw a live pitch. It just so happens that those things are amazing for TikTok. I guess it's true: the Bananas and TikTok are made for each other.

So how did we even get turned on to TikTok? That might be the funniest story of all.

Our social media coordinator, Savanah Alaniz—yes, that's her real first name—attended Texas A&M–Corpus Christi in 2019. One day, she noticed that a baseball player from her school reposted something from the Savannah Bananas. Savannah Bananas? Savanah Alaniz?

Like most people, she thought it was utter craziness—baseball players in kilts, crazy dances, fun stuff. So being a marketing major, she wondered if the Bananas had internships to offer, even though we were one thousand miles away.

After months of interviews, Savanah secured the internship and planned on starting in the spring of 2020, but COVID hit a month later, so she didn't arrive until the summer. She admitted later she was hesitant about what she was getting into and almost didn't show up. But when Savanah arrived, we immediately put her to work.

During the interview with Kara Heater, our marketing director, Savanah had been asked what she would do to help the Bananas' exposure. Her response: "I'd get you a TikTok. You guys would be perfect. I feel like it fits you."

The next day, Kara opened our TikTok account. Savanah told us later that she felt good about her internship chances when she saw the Bananas had immediately jumped on her TikTok suggestion.

When Savanah arrived in Savannah, the Bananas' TikTok account had 206 followers. Kara had posted six videos. We gave Savanah the TikTok password and said, "Go knock yourself out, kid."

She did.

Everyone was still on COVID lockdown, and her internship was to last three months. Savanah's first big hit was the Pose Challenge. We had photos of athletes throwing a baseball, then videos of them reenacting the play with a camera-flash effect to a song called "Hold That Pose." It took off. It got thirty thousand views. We hadn't seen that kind of response on any of our social media platforms.

Not long after that, I challenged her to post more often and try to get to ten thousand total followers by the end of the summer. Savanah later told me she called her mom and was freaked out because she didn't think ten thousand was possible, and she didn't want to let me down.

Our TikTok account got to ten thousand pretty quickly. So then it became, "What about twenty-five thousand?" We kept pushing. We didn't want to get comfortable. We had no real idea where this was going, but we weren't going to stop.

And that's the story of how we got to three million TikTok followers (and counting).

We hired Savanah full-time pretty quickly. She earned her college degree in the spring of 2022, not long after we finished our World Tour. If you ask me, I think she got her on-the-job doctorate in marketing long before that.

Savanah always thought her dream job would be in MLB. Regardless of what happens, she already found out the best part about Bananaland.

"I have the creative freedom to do whatever I want," Savanah said. "I don't just want to toe the line. I want to step three feet over it."

And so do our staff and our players. More and more, our players come up with cool video ideas because they love the feedback and the constant affirmations. In one of our funniest videos, Josh

Lavender approached the plate as a "golf batter." He studied home plate like it was the first tee at the Masters. He had a caddie and everything.

That idea came from our finance director.

Another time, Kara got one of our pitchers, Kyle Luigs, to ask our Instagram followers: "What crazy things do you want to see in our games?"

We had more than three hundred comments in a flash.

Pitch with your shoes off.

Do a cartwheel while you're running to first base.

Play Duck-Duck-Goose in the outfield.

We tried a few of the fans' ideas. They were good. And that's the whole idea of social media. It's about engagement. It's interaction with the fans.

Like Kara said, "This has blown up bigger than we ever could have imagined. We're getting fans involved in ways no other sports team ever has."

At a game in Daytona Beach, Savanah was sitting on a bench with the bleachers behind her. She was tweeting on her laptop. From behind, she heard someone say, "Oh my gosh! Is that the girl who does social media? Let's tweet at her and see if she sees it. I think we're watching her tweet right now."

Well, Savanah tweeted right back: "Hey, guys! If you're feeling generous, can you get me a bottle of water? I could really use one right now!"

They not only handed her a water bottle through the net, but they took a picture of Savanah drinking it and tweeted that out. And they said, "We love following you!"

Here's why that was important:

To them, Savanah was a celebrity. She *was* the Savannah Bananas. She not only recognized those fans but also responded to them. They all shared a fun little moment. The Savannah Bananas aren't some faceless corporate team that can't be touched. The Bananas are real people. Those fans felt *heard*.

Aren't people tired of those automated replies from big brands? That's as antiseptic as it gets. People share their lives with us because they know we care.

We had a fourteen-year-old girl following us on TikTok. She messaged, "Hey Bananas, I just got broken up with. What's the best way I should go about this?"

We came right back: "I don't know, girl. Grab some ice cream? Dance it out? Cry if you need to. It's not a bad thing."

Hey Bananas, I just had a baby!
Hey Bananas, I just graduated college!

It's so cool that people view us that way. They share life's big moments with family and friends but also with the Savannah Bananas. We work hard to create a brand voice that alternates between irreverent, sarcastic, funny, and caring—depending on the situation.

This is the future. The way we communicate is changing by the day, almost by the hour. That's a big part of why we created Banana Ball. When the younger generation grows up—after mostly watching baseball highlights, maybe, but never entire baseball games—what kind of fan following can baseball expect?

Somebody brought my attention to a conversation on the nationally syndicated *Dan Patrick Show* radio podcast. His guest was Mark Cuban, owner of the NBA's Dallas Mavericks and an investor on the *Shark Tank* ABC reality show, where prospective business entrepreneurs pitch their ideas to a team of business "sharks."

Mark Cuban said he felt baseball's older fan base didn't lend itself to social media, but the sport was really designed for a TikTok-style presentation that would complement linear television. For a small subscription, fans could have an algorithmically driven presentation that included their favorite players and teams.

Dan Patrick agreed and wondered why that wasn't obvious to baseball.

"That's a mystery I've never been able to follow," Cuban said.

We hear it and see it all the time.

In Daytona Beach, a middle school teacher told us he had found out about our World Tour on his TikTok feed.

In Birmingham, a fan had a poster board that rated our latest TikTok dances.

In Kansas City, Little League teams were doing TikTok dances before their Saturday-morning games.

Eric Byrnes, our coach, played in the big leagues. He worked for MLB Network. He has lived that life. And he sees a big problem down the line.

"There's a disconnect," Byrnesie said. "First and foremost, how can baseball improve fan engagement? MLB has always been like, *Well, here's the product.* That's not good enough anymore. It's too slow."

We believe the fans want fun.

That's why we send out a pitcher on stilts or a hitter with his bat on fire or a guy singing his walk-up song while playing the guitar. Those are incredible sights in the stadium, first and foremost, but they are equally amazing on a TikTok video.

And the dances? Fans love the dances. We call our choreographed numbers the 3-2-2—for the third inning, the second batter, and the second pitch. Typically, our pitchers, usually Kyle Luigs or Christian Dearman; our second baseman Dalton Mauldin; our shortstop Ryan Cox; and our centerfielder Reece Hampton are involved. Sometimes, the umpire, Vincent Chapman, is part of the gag.

"We've always had talented content people in place, but now it's off the charts," Kyle said. "The resources and the buy-in from people behind the curtain, that's what makes it go. The players get the praise. We put out these crazy dance videos. Then we're in a new city and kids who I've never met tell me I'm their favorite pitcher and they drove ten hours to see me play. They ask what dance we're doing tonight. It all just blows my mind."

With the help of our break-dancing first-base coach, Maceo Harrison, we always have a new dance ready. Players get the video to review a few days beforehand; then Maceo works to perfect it on game day.

We did "Let's Groove Tonight."

We did the Beyoncé drop challenge.

We did "Body on My Mind."

But the dance that got the most reaction was when we picked up Celine Dion's "It's All Coming Back to Me Now," a song that was trending on TikTok at the time.

Right when Celine belted out, "Baby . . . Baby . . . Baby . . . If you touch me like this . . . And when you hold me like that," a very dramatic Christian Dearman threw his cap and glove to the side, then ripped off his jersey and gripped the baseball like it was a microphone, lip-synching while shirtless. Then he delivered the pitch.

It was a swinging strike.

And the Daytona Beach crowd went wild, not to mention seventy million TikTok viewers over the next few days.

"It doesn't matter who does it first with TikTok," Savanah said. "One person does it and the others follow. We put a Banana spin on it. Then we'll see Little League teams trying to copy the things we do. Imitation is the most sincere form of flattery. Social media is a beast. You're constantly pushing stuff, trying something new. But that's who we are."

Savanah said she grew up wanting to become a third-grade teacher. Now she's part of a team that's teaching baseball fans how to have fun. I feel like we have so far to go. But even in the crazy new world of social media, we've already learned that creativity, fan engagement, and kindness can take us millions of miles. It might even give us the distinction of being "TikTok's Favorite Team."

Chapter Fifteen

The True Baseball Players

It blows me away that the Bananas have millions of worldwide fans—millions!—who love what we do. But we have skeptics, too. And this is what we hear:

"Yeah, yeah. We get it. The players sing and dance. You've got the guy on stilts. The trick pitchers. The guy who comes up with his bat on fire. The guys doing backflips all over the field. And that's all pretty cool.

"But how good is the actual baseball? Can these guys really play? Are they legitimate professional players or just clowns with gloves?"

Not only are they legitimate; they are flat-out amazing.

The grind of baseball is such that players need discipline and mental toughness to perform game after game. How they measure their days and keep to their schedules is important in a long season. Unlike football, which is regimented and scheduled to the second, with a weekly game to punctuate the preparation, baseball is a game of often monotonous repetition and the ability to produce over the long run, not just in short bursts. So the discipline and patience needed to navigate game after game are often the difference.

Banana Ball adds more twists. We ask our players to greet fans at the gate . . . maybe to pie somebody in the face as part of an on-field stunt . . . then dance with a young girl in the stands and present her a rose . . . then throw strikes . . . then dance to "Hey Baby" . . . then throw more strikes . . . then run up in the stands when we win an inning . . . then go out and parade with the fans after the game.

It's unbelievably different from anything they have ever experienced. Baseball players are accustomed to a measured schedule with downtime. Jumping between baseball and entertainment, sometimes on very short notice, can be jarring for players who have never been asked to be that versatile, but our teams make it work so beautifully. And they have a blast.

When Berry Aldridge, our baseball operations coordinator, came on as an intern in 2016, he was a hard-bitten baseball player. He played at Armstrong State. He'd been an old-school catcher and was the son of a coach. He's the type who doesn't display any crazy emotions, acts like he's been there before—the whole deal.

Berry started with our on-field promotions. And as he likes to remind us, in his trial by fire, we had him shaking his rear in a French maid outfit in front of a bunch of his friends in the stands. Why would any self-respecting baseball player subject himself to that?

Let Berry tell it: "You figure out real quick what your tolerance is for taking yourself seriously. I was not going to be the type of person who takes themselves so seriously. I've had great successes because of it in business and life. I'm so relaxed now. It's second nature to just be yourself. If you're authentic, you don't have to put on a front."

Berry is now the guy who helps identify potential players for the Bananas. He has a great eye. But one thing is certain: in searching for the right blend of talent and entertainment, we don't sacrifice the baseball skill.

When we had to decide which players would be Bananas and which ones would be Party Animals, our first priority was to make the teams as even as possible because we wanted competition. Other than that, you might say the Bananas are the kind of players you could bring home to meet your mother. The Party Animals were more like the scraggly antiheroes, the wrestling heels. It seems so cliché to describe it as "Good vs. Evil," but that's kind of the story line for our fans. And it works.

On our World Tour, we had Jake Skole, a first-round pick by the Texas Rangers. (You might recognize some other players who were taken in the 2010 first round: Bryce Harper, Manny Machado, Chris Sale, Christian Yelich, Noah Syndergaard.)

We had Michael Deeb, who played football at Notre Dame. We had Reece Hampton, one of the best center fielders I've ever seen, and shortstop Ryan Cox, an absolute magician with the glove.

We also had Christian Dearman, a strike-throwing machine. And we had Dakota McFadden, a six-foot-three, 240-pound beast who throws in the mid-nineties and can hit it out of any ballpark.

Most of those players were still chasing their baseball dreams, either in the independent leagues or affiliated ball. Why then would they play for the Bananas instead of staying on a track to shoot for the major leagues? What's in it for them, other than some at bats?

Somebody asked that of Dakota McFadden, one of our most talented players. All he did was smile.

"You don't get an experience like this more than once in a lifetime," Dakota said. "It makes baseball fun."

The players have been under intense pressure their whole lives. Banana Ball is wonderful and unique, even for players who can compete at higher levels and might have a shot at the majors. Our games are a cool niche. The really smart guys recognize that opportunity.

That's why, if you ask me, we should put Bill LeRoy and Kyle Luigs on our Bananas Mount Rushmore. These are the guys who truly get it.

Bill and Kyle are part players, coaches, front-office employees, equipment managers, groundskeepers, and counselors. And they're all Bananas.

They played together at the University of North Georgia and were looking for a college summer team. Some people might watch Kyle as a pitcher and Bill as a catcher and think, *OK, nothing special*, because they don't appear to be unusually talented. We think they're *extremely* special. They are also Bananas role models.

It's typical to see Bill and Kyle cleaning up the clubhouse, helping with the field, organizing our summer camp, or showing the way for a young player. When Adam Virant, our Party Animals manager, flew back from New York for one of our World Tour games, it was a two-hour wait for an Uber, so Viro called Kyle to tell him he wouldn't be able to get to the stadium immediately. With no hesitation, Kyle dropped everything and picked up Viro at the airport. It takes an army to put on a Bananas game, and we don't have an army. But with selfless guys like Bill and Kyle to set the example, things run pretty well in Bananaland.

When Bill and Kyle first showed up to the college team, they weren't exactly first options. I'm not sure they were second, third, or fourth options. They were good players. So what sets them apart? As they say, the best ability is availability. A great attitude doesn't hurt. Then, they combined baseball ability with an understanding of what the Bananas are all about, plus the willingness to try just about anything while setting an example for the other players.

After his freshman season, Bill went back to his hometown of Dublin, Georgia, a tiny town that has little more than an intersection with a Love's Travel Stop. He did some landscaping, but after a couple of days in the hundred-degree heat, summer ball looked pretty good. At least most of the baseball would be under the lights—and far from the ten-hour workdays lugging fifty-pound bags of sod or shoveling rocks in the unbearable humidity. Their North Georgia coach recommended Bill and Kyle for our college team.

Well, we look at a lot of guys. They said later they thought it was a one-week contract. It was actually a two-day fill-in spot. They showed up without really knowing what they were getting into. In most cases, these guys would not have lasted very long. There are only a few reasons why people are still reading about Bill LeRoy and Kyle Luigs.

They had great attitudes. They were great teammates. They put down their pride and embraced the Bananas.

"I didn't even know who the Bananas were," Bill said. "And I was pretty much out the door after a few days. But I decided to go all-in, work hard, be a leader, do what they ask, although I had never seen any baseball like this before. What did I have to lose?"

The team's newest player arrived in the dugout wearing his uniform and tennis shoes instead of cleats. When he saw his name in the starting lineup that first evening, a shocked Bill ran back into the locker room to change into his cleats. Bill realized a spectacular entrance would be memorable, so he rode into the stadium on a military truck, wearing a SWAT helmet. He looked the part—and got two hits. Two days later, we signed Bill to a full contract. Now we can't imagine the Bananas without him.

Every game, he waves his arms into a clap above his head, exciting the crowd as he gyrates to "The Stroke" by Billy Squier. Instead of waiting to be introduced, Bill grabs the microphone and introduces himself.

"Ladies and gentlemen, put your hands together. Now batting, from the big town of Dublin, Georgia, number one, University of North Georgia alumni . . . myself," he shouts, stretching out the word before shouting, "Bill LeRoy."

Bill and Kyle are inseparable. They shared a dorm room in college. Now they're in their third house together, a short walk from Grayson Stadium. They could do a how-to video on succeeding with the Bananas—with entertainment, hard work, a fans-first approach, and great baseball.

On the mound, Kyle is always up for a cool dance routine—or any video. I still laugh about the *Baywatch* skit he and Bill and a few of the other guys did on the beach at Tybee Island. Another night, our video team captured Kyle's intimate table for two at the ballpark and a dinner date . . . with a five-year-old.

"We like to have fun," Kyle said. "But with all the showmanship stuff we do, the baseball sometimes gets overlooked. People say, 'Do these guys even play real baseball? They wouldn't stand a chance against real competition.' That's far from the truth. We may do crazy stuff, but we can play. On our World Tour, those were some of the most talented players I've ever seen."

Even as a baby my dad presented me as a "showman." Jesse Cole

Sitting next to Red Sox closer Lee Smith as honorary batboy for the Red Sox. Jesse Cole

Dad and I traveled all over the country playing baseball—here we are when I was thirteen years old in Oklahoma at the AAU National tournament.

Jesse Cole

Pitching at Wofford College my
sophomore year, in Spartanburg,
South Carolina. <small>JESSE COLE</small>

With Amelia Red in our
Children's Theatre production
of *Go to Bed, Amelia Red.*
<small>JESSE COLE</small>

Emily and I working with the Gastonia
Grizzlies. <small>JESSE COLE</small>

Emily rocking the hot dog costume promoting the team in Martinsville, Virginia. JESSE COLE

My dad joined in on the fun for a Pie Your Son promotion with the Gastonia Grizzlies.
KEITH COWARD/*SPORTSPAGE MAGAZINE*

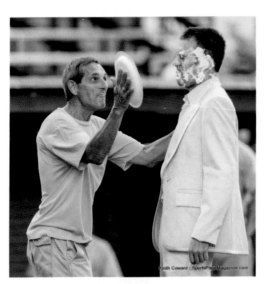

August 4, 2014: the night I proposed to Emily in front of a sold-out crowd in Gastonia. JOSH TEEPLE PHOTOGRAPHY

October 10, 2015: getting married in the rain at our ballpark in Gastonia. JESSE COLE

October 5, 2015: Our first day in the office in Savannah was not ideal. Here President Jared Orton works on a table we found, amidst cut phone lines and internet lines. JESSE COLE

Our air bed that Emily and I slept on after having to sell our house. JESSE COLE

Fans finally went Bananas and started wearing costumes to every game. MALCOLM TULLY, SAVANNAH BANANAS

Emily and I holding the CPL Petitt Cup after winning the CPL championship in our first season.
Jesse Cole

Fun day in the office where we all dressed up as other coworkers. This was in the third trimester of Emily's pregnancy with Maverick, so I went all out. Jesse Cole

Introducing the Banana Baby for Opening Day of the 2018 season, our son, Maverick Cole. Emily wasn't thrilled with the idea and the promotion, as Maverick was only twenty-four days old!
Malcolm Tully, Savannah Bananas

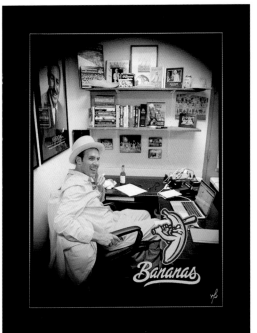

In my old office, where a lot of the inspiration came in the early days.
MIL CANNON

"Hey Baby" with a sold-out Bananas crowd will always be my favorite promotion and dance during Bananas shows.   MALCOLM TULLY, SAVANNAH BANANAS

Postgame plaza party with all the players and characters.

MALCOLM TULLY, SAVANNAH BANANAS

Christian Dearman getting an autograph from a young fan.

STAN GROSSFELD/THE BOSTON GLOBE

Head Coach Tyler Gillum and I before another Bananas show.

Malcolm Tully, Savannah Bananas

Bill LeRoy busting a move with the Banana Nanas.

Malcolm Tully, Savannah Bananas

Another fan trying to get tickets to a sold-out Bananas show.

Maverick rocking a yellow tux before a Bananas game after his first birthday.

Pregame with the Banana Pep Band.

The electric Eric Byrnes, the Bananas head coach of the 2022 Banana Ball World Tour. Malcolm Tully, Savannah Bananas

March 11, 2022: "I Wanna Dance with Somebody," players and Maceo went all out in kilts for the first game of the 2022 Banana Ball World Tour. Malcolm Tully, Savannah Bananas

March 12, 2022: second game of the 2022 Banana Ball World Tour. Rare freezing temperatures couldn't keep thousands of fans from arriving early to see the Opening March and "Hey Baby."

MALCOLM TULLY, SAVANNAH BANANAS

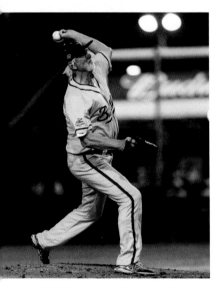

Postgame "Stand by Me" with the cast and fans in Daytona after our first stop on the 2022 World Tour in Daytona.

HUNTER CONE, SAVANNAH BANANAS

Bill "Spaceman" Lee pitching in Daytona on the Banana Ball World Tour.

HUNTER CONE, SAVANNAH BANANAS

The entire Bananas cast posing before a tour stop in Montgomery, Alabama.

Dakota "Stilts" Albritton making his pitching debut in Columbus, Georgia.

Bringing Banana Ball to the oldest ballpark in America: Rickwood Field, Birmingham, Alabama.

HUNTER CONE, SAVANNAH BANANAS

"Hey Baby" on night two at Legends Field in Kansas City after the fans rushed the gates for our game against the Kansas City Monarchs.

HUNTER CONE, SAVANNAH BANANAS

(below) The "Thunderstuck" kickline before the game against the Monarchs.   HUNTER CONE, SAVANNAH BANANAS

May 24, 2022: first Banana Fest Banana Ball game where we broke the record for most fans in banana costumes.   MALCOLM TULLY, SAVANNAH BANANAS

August 5, 2022: the last time Emily and I would ever hold the CPL Petitt Cup trophy, after winning back-to-back CPL championships. Two weeks later, we would announce we are leaving the CPL and going all-in on Banana Ball.   MALCOLM TULLY, SAVANNAH BANANAS

Emily and I posing for ESPN Media Day.

MICHAEL GALINSKY

The final shot for ESPN Media Day with the cast of Bananaland.
MICHAEL GALINSKY

September 27, 2022: Emily and I on the field at Fenway after meeting with the Red Sox about bringing Banana Ball to Boston.
JESSE COLE

The Bananas' best player in terms of pure talent would easily be Jake Skole. It's easy to see why he was a first-round draft pick. He has such a sweet swing, great power, and a big arm; he also covers ground in the outfield. Like everyone in baseball, he has a story. One question follows him everywhere: "Why didn't you make the major leagues?"

Jake was supposed to be a baseball and football player at Georgia Tech, but when the Rangers selected him fifteenth overall and they offered him a $1.557 million signing bonus, he made the decision to turn pro. Like any big-time college baseball player drafted out of high school, he planned to play in the big leagues for twenty years.

Plans don't always work. Jake never got underway with the Rangers. The team drafted him because he was a fast leadoff-type player. He got bigger because they tried to make him a power guy. Somewhere along the line, he lost his identity and couldn't get out of the minors. He was traded to the Yankees but found himself behind other prospects there.

In desperation, the Yankees batting coach asked Jake to try the batting stance he used in high school, an attempt to make him comfortable. Jake froze up. The high school version of Jake Skole? He couldn't even remember that guy. Nearly six years had passed since he had been drafted. His confidence was gone. He had a label—a first-rounder who didn't make it. Jake asked for his release so he could play college football.

I give Jake a ton of credit for reinventing himself. He signed with the University of Georgia, mostly playing as a backup safety and special teams guy. During his years at Georgia, he got big-time SEC experience and played in a national title game. He also earned his degree.

After college, Jake built a lucrative career in real estate but still had the baseball itch. Our coaches knew that. When we called him on a whim, Jake was excited to try the Bananas.

"I think I got chewed up by the expectations," Jake said. "What eighteen-year-old can truly handle all of that? With the Bananas, it's probably the first time I've played without pressure since Little League. Every organization should try to create an atmosphere like the Bananas have. It's huge."

Jake pushed himself out of his comfort zone and played a World Wrestling Entertainment–type role when he was introduced. He flexed, ripped off his jersey, and went to the plate shirtless. In his first time at bat, he slammed a hit up the middle. When he rounded first base, I could see him smile, and I knew he had found his love for the game again. As interesting as it was to say we had a former baseball draft pick and Georgia Bulldog football player on our Bananas team, Jake wasn't our only player who had starred on a football field. We also had Michael Deeb, of Notre Dame. He played in the Orange Bowl and was part of some big-time teams. But when injuries ended his football career, he rejoined baseball as a graduate transfer to Bethune-Cookman.

"I wouldn't trade that experience for the world," Michael said. "At Cookman, a lot of times, I was the only white guy in a class. People wanted to know who I was, what I was doing there. I met a lot of people who grew up differently than I did. You come to find out that people are a lot more similar than they are different."

Michael signed with the White Sox, but he was injured when COVID-19 hit. The ChiSox were downsizing and released Michael. The Bananas became his platform for jump-starting his baseball passion again. But we were all touched by his love of people—especially young people.

Michael grew up in South Florida and still remembers going to a Miami game when he was ten years old and Miguel Cabrera was with the Marlins. "Miggy" gave Michael the thrill of his young life when he pointed to Michael in the stands to single him out for a game of catch.

"Why can't all athletes do that?" Michael said. "It doesn't take much to put a smile on a kid's face. It's the coolest thing about the Bananas, the way we interact with fans. I'm going to frame my jersey with all the autographs and keep it forever. To have the ability to potentially impact the life of a kid, it's incredible. It's beyond sports. It's life. It matters. Playing baseball is fleeting."

I love that perspective. I can relate after having my college baseball career taken away by injury. Christian Dearman, one of our true Bananas stars, nearly had the same kind of experience.

Christian was pitching at Tallahassee Community College in Florida, about to close out a game, when he heard a pop. It was a torn latissimus dorsi tendon, something the medical world had rarely seen at the time. The doctor told him to forget about baseball because he wouldn't be able to ever use his arm again at full strength.

Knowing Christian like I do now, I can easily visualize him taking that as a pure challenge. Sure enough, by the next year, he was back to pitching and wound up finishing his college career at St. Thomas University. We're grateful he heard about the Bananas and joined us. He's such a ham. It was the perfect fit.

He's comfortable being uncomfortable. He's up for anything.

"What kind of life do you want to live?" Christian said. "Do you want to enjoy life or do you just want to walk through it? If you want me to dance to 'YMCA,' I'll do it. If you want me to dress up like Little Bo-Peep, I'll do it. I never thought I could have this much fun at baseball.

"The kids are the best part. They say, 'The Bananas are always smiling and happy. The other ballplayers blow us off, but you guys care.' That just makes my heart sing. I like being a role model."

Dakota McFadden grew to love that role, too. When Dakota played for the Bananas, he could always be spotted down the right-field line before a game, drawing something in the dirt, then pointing to the sky. It turns out he has lost some special people in his life—a couple of teammates, a childhood friend, a coach, a kid who looked up to him. He writes down their baseball numbers or their initials and says a little prayer before giving thanks for his opportunities.

"When I look into the faces of the kids watching our games and smiling, I see my friends," Dakota said. "I know that our time is limited here. It's amazing that we can make people smile and entertain them.

"I'm still amazed by the kids who call out to me and they actually know my name. They see us as heroes. That feeling, you can never get rid of it. We have to keep that spirit going. The Bananas are not about us. The Bananas are about them."

Dakota is one of the most talented baseball players I've ever seen. I appreciate his skill. Even more, I appreciate his ability to go all-in for our fans and be an entertainer. He's a big, intimidating-looking guy when you first spot him. Then when he smiles, it's electrifying. The fans love him.

And we can't talk about talent without mentioning Dan Oberst. Dan may be the best hitter I've ever seen in Savannah, and he turned down an independent league contract after college to stay with the Bananas and help us win a championship. He's been so important for us.

I hope all our guys keep chasing baseball dreams. But if they go to other teams, I hope they bring the Bananas' spirit with them. It's always good to put the fans first.

Bill LeRoy once said something that stuck with me. Along with every Bananas player—including myself—Bill dreamed of playing in the major leagues. If that never happens, Bill said, every player's former self should be so proud of what we're all doing with the Bananas.

And sometimes, dreams can change.

"We're obviously competitive in baseball, but not to the point where it's taking away from our joy of the game and the joy of being around people," Bill said.

Can these guys play good baseball? Absolutely.

But they can do a lot more, too. And that's why the fans love them so much.

Chapter Sixteen

Entertainers

With the Savannah Bananas, we expect great ballplayers. But that's just the beginning. What makes the difference is great entertainment, unusual skills, and master showmanship.

"I've never seen that on a baseball field."

That's a typical reaction for the Bananas organization to hear from its fans. The thing is, we never know if the fan is referring to our players' stellar baseball ability or their over-the-top antics, which we don't consider over-the-top. Either way, we call them Bananas.

Ever seen a guy who could pitch, bat, or play first base—on stilts? Introducing Dakota Albritton. We call him "Stilts."

How about an entire lineup wearing kilts? Stilts and kilts? The Bananas have been known to combine the two disciplines.

I've mentioned that we have a tough-looking power hitter coming to the plate with his bat on fire. Literally on fire? Yes. Flaming. Meet hot-hitting Zak Whalin.

It would be quite a gimmick for a musician to play his own walk-up song, then trade his guitar for a bat before smacking a single up the middle. We have that guy, too. We give you the talented Dalton Mauldin.

Then there's the only guy in baseball dressed like a rodeo clown who throws strikes behind his back or through his legs, then delivers another pitch after doing a cartwheel. That's our Mat Wolf.

What kind of madness is this?

Welcome to Bananaland.

This is the personification of my personal slogan. *Stop standing still. Start standing out.* With the Bananas, our goal is to be the fastest-paced, most entertaining brand of baseball ever seen. If we can push the boundaries even more with the craziest skills out there, we're going to stand out.

We ask for specifics on our tryout form: What are your special talents? Tell us how you would stage your special entrance to the field. We ask for a video to show something that sets you apart. The video is a good screening tool for us, usually helping us decide whether we want to move forward. Of course, we want them to dress for success, so we ask them to wear something that will make us take notice.

The Bananas organization believes in giving our players creative license on the front end, and we're constantly surprised what they've been able to come up with. We get players who can juggle. Some can manipulate their gloves and bats like they are magicians. Traditional players have constantly been told to act like they have been there before. Instead of flair, fun, joyfulness, and uniqueness, it's fundamentals, fundamentals, fundamentals. There's a perception that flair and celebrating are making it all about the individual, not the team, so they're frowned upon. Players have creativity beaten out of them, and they are hesitant to try anything that looks different, but we found that when we let them loose, they generate ideas, fun, and excitement.

That's how Zak Whalin came up with the idea of a flaming bat.

What an incredible visual. I've seen it on posters before, you know, the big-time player and hot hitter with flames coming from the barrel. It's a really cool photo. But I had never seen it in real time or in a game.

Until Zak Whalin blew us all away with his idea. It was opening day for Major League Baseball. And what was number one that night on ESPN's top ten plays? It was Zak Whalin coming to the plate at a Bananas game with his bat on fire! People lost their minds. That thing blew up beyond belief, and it was still being talked about throughout 2022.

We had brought Zak to our team in 2021 because other players had moved to independent league teams and we needed a catcher for our games in Mobile. He came highly recommended because he hit close to .400 in junior college and at Central Missouri. We told Zak he needed a nickname. He thought about it a minute; then his eyes lit up when he proclaimed, "I'm the Mild Thing." Not "Wild Thing." He was the "Mild Thing." That made us laugh. His hitting ability and his defensive skills behind the plate definitely put him on our list as a player to watch for our 2022 World Tour tryouts.

Berry Aldridge, our baseball operations coordinator, knew the bar was climbing higher for tryouts, so he challenged Zak to put on a show by coming up with a gimmick, showing off a skill, or performing a magic trick.

Zak was nervous for weeks because he knew he'd be competing against some big personalities and a lot of general craziness. Berry said he texted Zak to ask him his plan.

Maybe Zak hadn't thought it through, and maybe he wasn't completely serious, but he texted back, "I'll light my bat on fire."

Berry had a quick response:

"That would be sweet!"

Once Zak made the team—we put him on the Party Animals because he looked the part—he started experimenting. How was he actually going to come up with his bat on fire? Gasoline wasn't going to work because it sinks into the wood and stays on fire, and we didn't want that. Zak tried some mixtures of lighter fluid. He finally found a charcoal lighter fluid with an oily residue that burned itself out, but he discovered he couldn't light it with a match or lighter because neither generated enough heat. Fortunately, he found a solution before game time.

We wanted to try it in Daytona Beach, at the first stop, but they were a little nervous about their turf field going up in flames. We went back and forth and finally decided it would be cool to unveil it in Savannah. We wouldn't announce it in advance so we could have maximum shock value.

Zak had to time it just right, so ten seconds before he was announced, he slapped on the fluid and whipped out a blowtorch and lit up the bat.

Looking like a badass, Zak strode from the on-deck circle to the plate with his bat smoldering, then (metaphorically) lit up the pitcher with a single up the middle on the first pitch. The crowd went nuts.

After his big swing, Zak dropped the bat in the infield dirt, safely snuffing out the flames. The sight of the bat on fire, and the fact that Zak got a base hit, remains one of the coolest stunts Bananaland has ever seen.

But the real show had just started.

After the game, someone from Zak's hometown of Fort Myers,

Florida, said he was on the local news. His family in Ohio and California called to say the same thing. The ESPN app sent the video clip all over the world, and by the time Zak went to bed, it had gotten 800,000 views. By lunchtime the next day, it was up to three million. Seven other clips from MLB's opening day made ESPN's top ten, but Zak was number one.

The viral response mystified Zak.

"I didn't expect that reaction," Zak said. "It was supposed to be a one-off. Next thing I know, I'm being interviewed by *TMZ*. I'm in the *New York Post*. I'm the flaming-bat guy. I'm usually such a goofball, but this was something completely different.

"I couldn't even fathom this happening in MLB. If you tried it in a minor-league game, they'd probably eject you and you'd be ostracized. With the Bananas, it's fun. People like to see other people having fun. I think we're giving fans what they truly want—fun. You're always going to see something crazy at a Bananas game."

A guy playing baseball on stilts also qualifies as crazy.

Dakota Albritton showed up at our tryouts with his unicycle. He also had a pair of stilts.

"You have stilts?" I said. "You think you can hit on them?"

"I don't see why not," Stilts said.

Why would he have ever tried such a thing? In fact, he hadn't used the stilts in about ten years, ever since he'd received them as a Christmas gift. After leaving them untouched in his shed for that long, he finally pulled them out again when his mom, who helped him with his tryout application package, wrote down "walking on stilts" as one of his "weird talents." By the time he brought them to the tryout, they were so old and the straps had become so brittle that he had to initially secure them to his legs with dog collars.

When Stilts takes the field, adult fans' jaws drop and younger fans' eyes light up. It is an amazing sight. Our umpire has to stand on a step stool while he views Stilts's strike zone.

When Stilts is on the mound, batters flinch because they find it a little intimidating to pick up a fastball that's coming in from the angle of an arm that's ten feet high.

It's hilarious to watch Stilts get ready because each pair of stilts weighs about fifteen pounds and he has to pull on his extralong baseball pants over them. He has to fully step out of the dugout to stand up, and it's a startling sight at first for the folks in the front rows.

Stilts said he keeps getting the same question: Why?

"My answer is always the same: Why not?" Stilts said. "It obviously draws attention. That's what we're all about, making people happy, making them smile, making them laugh.

"I see myself in every kid. That used to be me out there. I never thought I could bring this much joy and happiness to kids. I'm going to keep doing it. It doesn't take much to make me happy."

Stilts is from Ellaville, Georgia, a one-stoplight, zero-McDonald's town of about eighteen hundred people. He used to skin deer for a living. Now he builds dog kennels and chicken coops. His parents say Stilts has always been a daredevil. He's broken eight limbs and had staples in his head after falling out of a tree.

What's he scared of?

"Spiders and the good Lord . . . that's about it."

He sure isn't scared of playing baseball on stilts, even though his fiancée, Haley Nutt, still cringes from time to time.

Haley said Stilts is just one of those adrenaline junkies, a lover of danger, a guy who tries just about anything for a rush. Stilts says playing baseball on stilts is probably one of the least dangerous things he has ever attempted . . . which makes me wonder what else he *has* tried . . . but we love having him on the Bananas.

During tryouts, Stilts stood on the outfield warning track, towering over the fence. Our broadcast entertainer, Biko Skalla, was interviewing Stilts while bouncing on a trampoline on the other side of the fence, timing each question for the apex of his jump when he could make eye contact.

He's different and he's entertaining, and fans love watching a ten-foot-tall right-hander who consistently nails the strike zone. Stilts stands out. That makes him the perfect Banana.

Dalton Mauldin, our second baseman, is a pretty scrappy in-fielder who also gets big hits, but he has another legit talent.

How many baseball players have written and recorded their own walk-up song? Dalton did. He's a singer/songwriter, and when he comes up to the plate, we play "That's How It Goes," the song he released before our World Tour.

Dalton strummed his guitar as he brought it to the plate, then traded it for a bat. One time, he came up doing "Sweet Caroline," and on the chorus, instead of "Dum-Dum-Dum," he sang, "Ba-Nan-A."

Dalton played college baseball, finishing up at Trevecca Naza-rene in Nashville; he now lives part-time in Nashville, where he's part of the music scene. We're hoping he makes it big and that playing for the Bananas helps him gain exposure.

Trying to make it in baseball parallels trying to make it in music. Sometimes, things hit just right, but there is a ton of ex-perimentation and struggles. Dalton can exist successfully in both worlds. His onstage background makes him a sophisticated performer for the Bananas. He's usually involved in the dance numbers with our pitchers, so he has been in the middle of our most popular videos.

He also performed in one of my favorite spots. At Daytona Beach, we wanted to capture something special in the locker room, that last bit of inspiration before taking the field. Dalton suggested "Centerfield," that baseball classic from John Fogerty. That was OK, but I was really feeling "Eye of the Tiger"—but as a slow, sappy ballad.

Dalton played it perfectly, drawing out every word, playing it straight. We even included some shots of his teammates waving their iPhone flashlights or emotionally dabbing their eyes. It was classic.

"Music is like my sixth baseball tool," Dalton said. "I feel like I can bring skills and abilities and contribute to the fan engagement and the on-field product. I get to reach a new demographic, and I'm engaging with fans organically. It's a win-win.

"Anytime I get a nod from Jesse, I feel like I'm doing something right. He has such an eye for what's right and what's going to work."

Well, I try. And we're always on the lookout for unusual skills.

It didn't take much thought to realize that Malachi Mitchell, maybe the fastest player in baseball, would be an asset for the Bananas. His dad is Dennis Mitchell, a former US Olympic track-and-field athlete who won a gold medal. Malachi certainly has great bloodlines. He goes from home to first base in 3.4 seconds, so he really flies. I've never seen a faster runner, although they said Deion Sanders got to first in 3.33 seconds. So Malachi is worth the price of admission and—as a bonus—he also does backflips.

We came across Alex Ziegler, the Bat Trick Guy, on YouTube and TikTok. Once I saw how he could spin a bat and step up to the plate while balancing it on his chin, I knew he would make a great Banana. He can whip the bat around his back, then between his legs, spinning, twisting, almost making the bat look like it's bending because it's going so fast. Oh, and he can do it all blindfolded.

"I can't say there's a demand for what I do, but people love it," said Alex, who was performing his bat tricks for fun on social media. "It's entertaining."

One of our most entertaining players is Mat Wolf, a thirty-four-year-old fourth-generation firefighter from Oklahoma City. He's a trick pitcher who does cartwheels, throws behind his back, tosses through his legs, all while dressed as a rodeo clown. Before he joined the organization, he had been coaching, but he'd also messed around with trick plays for years.

We couldn't wait to see him at tryouts, but Mat almost no-showed.

"I had the dream and a very unique skill set, but I was real uncertain about it," Mat said.

Thank goodness for Mat's wife, Magean, a former college softball player who played at Oklahoma City University, the 2012 National Association of Intercollegiate Athletics (NAIA) national champion runner-up. She was the quiet chatter in Mat's ear. Mat worried he was too old. He thought his style was too unorthodox. He didn't trust his skills and worried about his showmanship.

Magean reassured him and told him he would be a natural. Boy, she was right.

I won't forget the look of shock on Mat's face after he made the Bananas before the World Tour, because he hadn't believed it was going to happen. When it did, he was concerned about asking for time off from the fire station, and he didn't want to leave Magean and their two-year-old daughter, Raylee, behind.

Mat's fire station gave him the time off. We brought them all to Savannah, and it became a family adventure. By the time our World Tour had finished, it was downright unforgettable.

Mat wore a taped-down index card on his arm that listed each of his twenty-four pitches—the Blinder, the Panty Dropper, the Banana Split, the Spin-O-Rama, the Double Prosthetic, the D-Ball Special, the Showstopper, the Donkey Kong, the Houdini, the Split Single Axle, the Quick Slide, Around the Town, the Back-Door Roller Coaster, the Submarine, the Down to Up, the Satchel to Satchel, the Goose Tatum, the Price Is Right, the Keanon/Kyle, the Pop-N-Lock, the Mageanator, the Professor, the Right-Handed from the Left Side, and the Runaway Bride.

Most top major-league pitchers have three reliable pitches, maybe four.

Other players still stopped to watch Mat warm up in the bull-pen and deliver his crazy pitches. That was a show in itself. At times, he simply couldn't believe he was getting the chance to perform in seven cities before seventy thousand fans, and millions more online. Magean always believed.

Next to seventy-five-year-old Bill Lee, Mat was our oldest team member and one of the few with a young child. Mat said he kept thinking about that movie *The Rookie*, where Dennis Quaid played Jim Morris, the high school coach who gave baseball one more shot because his players insisted. Because Mat was a former high school coach in Oklahoma, the life he was living sounded a lot like that improbable story. Of course, Jim Morris made it to the major leagues.

"It's just nuts that I'm even here," Mat said. "My wife kept saying the Bananas perfectly fit my personality because I like to have fun and be goofy. I'm out here for the fun of the game. But I wouldn't even be here if my wife was negative about it or even neutral."

When they first met, Mat and Magean went out to a country bar with friends. Mat was too shy to dance, but Magean insisted.

She said he turned out to be the best dancer she'd ever seen. "He didn't want to show it," Magean said. "Mat has all the skill at things. I don't have as much skill, but I have the confidence, so we balance each other out. The Bananas just turned out to be an absolute blast, and we've got some stories to tell Raylee one day."

And boy, do they. Early on the tour, Magean was goofing around and threw some pitches in the bullpen, and our coaches noticed she had a pretty decent arm. She kept working at it with the fleeting thought that she might get into a game. It seemed like a long shot. But we're the Bananas. Is *anything* a long shot? When we were in Columbus, Georgia, and Mat Wolf came out of the game after two innings, we sent out a reliever—his wife.

Mat moved behind the plate and caught Magean. When she struck out a Party Animal batter, it was too perfect. Mat ran to the mound and kissed her. More Bananas history: baseball's first husband-wife combination.

Sometimes, it all comes together in priceless ways. A pitcher on stilts. A hitter with his bat on fire. A musician strumming his walk-on song on a guitar. The fastest man in baseball. A guy balancing a bat on his chin. A trick-pitcher-turned-catcher suddenly catching pitches from his wife.

That's what we're after.

That's entertainment.

Even more, that's Banana Ball.

Chapter Seventeen

Ideas

The Savannah Bananas *love* ideas.

We even love bad ideas. Frequently, bad ideas can lead to great ideas. I have come up with a ton of bad ideas all on my own—I might hold the world record for rotten ideas. But when we start kicking things around, when we get in a room and bounce things off one another, many ideas are not going to be great. Usually, out of every ten ideas we throw out, only one or two could potentially be something special.

As is true for baseball, success with idea generation is about volume. It's about taking your hacks every day. Over the course of a year, all our great ideas will get attention, and nobody will even know about the bad ideas we never tried.

We all have idea muscles. Like any other muscle, they need to be worked out regularly. That means getting to the gym, hitting the pavement, or simply establishing a workout routine. Regular workouts tone and strengthen muscles, and when a person starts missing workouts, it shows. When I don't give my idea muscles workouts, brainstorming and generating ideas on a regular basis,

I don't feel like my creative juices are flowing properly. My idea muscles feel soft and out of shape.

When ideas start flowing, I am energized and excited. Remember, nothing happens without the initial idea. That's the spark to get things going. When I worked with the Gastonia Grizzlies, I had an idea box. I wrote my ideas down on paper—notebook paper, old mailing envelopes, napkins, and anything else that happened to be handy when one came into my head—and kept them in this old box. That box was more valuable to me than currency because it held my ideas. I kept that box on my nightstand, so if the house ever burned down, that would be the first thing I saved.

I still have the idea box—it maybe cost a buck, and it's just a little wood-colored carton—but it has given way to an idea book, and I usually keep it next to me at all times. I start a new idea book every year, and I keep the old ones in my office for reference.

It's a pretty simple little book—hardback, leather-bound, nothing really that special-looking. Every morning, first thing without fail, I write down ten ideas. It's an idea-palooza. Some of them are terrible, but I'm constantly stimulating my mind and asking the same questions: *How can we make baseball fun? How can we do something that has never been done on a baseball field?*

I'll work on ideas in my office at home, or I'll take my idea book to the hotel when I travel. Sometimes in the morning, I'll read a little bit for some creative inspiration, but then I go right into the ideas.

I've learned that the best way is to go with a theme that I've started from the day before. Before I go to bed, I will write down where to start for the next day. Maybe it's pregame, or team parade promotions, or halftime shows, or postgame, or tour stops. It might be the craziest places to play a baseball game. It could be ways to celebrate a birthday. I come up with a theme, it's ready for me in the morning, and I just go.

People always ask me, "Do you come up with ideas in your sleep, then wake up at three in the morning and write them down?" It doesn't really go like that. I sleep through the night because I go pretty hard every day, and I need that sleep. I never use an alarm. I've never had a cup of coffee in my life. When I wake up at four thirty or five each morning, my mind switches on, and I'm ready to go.

The ideas are the most important part of my day. I know how my day is going to go based on the creativity of the ideas. If I struggle with an idea session, it's tough for me to get out of that. But if I have a few good ideas, and the creative juices are flowing, I feel that energy throughout the day. It's like a workout. When my idea muscle is flexing, I feel really good.

Every Monday, some of our creative staff gets together for our "Over the Top" (OTT) session. We don't hold back. That's where we can really get into Walt Disney's concept of plussing, where you keep building on ideas until they become great.

Generally, it's Zack Frongillo on the whiteboard at the stadium club. It's usually myself, Kara Heater, Savanah Alaniz, and Ivan Traczuk, our director of creative content. We have our buckets, similar to idea themes, and we just start throwing out ideas. Everybody has to come up with ideas for each bucket. If we get these crazy reactions and animated responses, that's when we know we're headed in the right direction. If there's a lot of pausing and stammering and quiet, then we're stuck.

We are never afraid of bad ideas. I mean, never. Anything to get the flow going. Like we've said before, bad ideas usually lead to good ideas. We'll just yell out a category—hitting entrances, scoring celebrations, three-two-two, dugout shenanigans, pregame

videos, creative dances—and you get your mind racing with anything that sounds good.

"So this has to be really big because it's Banana Fest."

"Everybody has to be involved."

"OK, let's have everyone do the Harlem Shake."

"How do we get it started?"

"It only works if everyone in the stadium is wearing a Banana
costume."

"What? Everyone?"

"How do we get the costumes to the fans?"

"Can you imagine how that would look?"

"Who's doing the dancing?"

"What do you mean? Everyone in the whole stadium is dancing."

It's such a fun, creative process. In many business settings,
people are hesitant to speak up. They keep great ideas to themselves. More than ever, you should never be afraid to get people's
attention. You've got to do it to stand out because it's a noisy
world out there.

Too many businesses and teams focus so much on sales revenue and driving growth, and those are fine things. But ideas
spur passion—and more ideas.

Sometimes, we remind ourselves what business we're in so we
can reconnect with our "why." The Bananas are in the entertainment business, and as a result, we have to be dramatically different. So the idea-palooza and OTT meetings are vital for us. That's
where we invented the Banana-Nanas senior-citizen dance team
and our Man-Nanas dad-bod cheerleading squad. It's how we
came up with our break-dancing first-base coach and the fash-
ionable idea to play in kilts for our Saint Patrick's Day game.

The OTT meeting can be pure madness—and I mean that in
the best way possible. We had one of the local sports reporters,

Nathan Dominitz of the *Savannah Morning News*, visit to research a story on how we operate and generate ideas in the OTT meetings. After the meeting, he walked out of the office, shaking his head as he commented, "I've never seen anything like that building of ideas."

That is definitely the start. Thinking even bigger is the next step. Walt Disney didn't believe in thinking outside the box. He never believed in having a box.

I love hearing how our staff members react to the OTT experience.

"You can completely suss out an idea, and nobody's going to look at you weird," said Kara Heater, our marketing director. "Well, they might look at you weird, but then they'll go, 'Wow! That's a good idea!' The whole thing is so fun. It makes it a thrilling, rewarding place to work."

I think it speaks to the environment we try to create. Everyone can have a great idea. We want to nurture those ideas and help them grow. When everyone feels like they can contribute to the larger goals, they get excited to come to work each day. It's an adventure. It's fun. When you have that attitude, it's not work. It's your passion.

"Jesse truly doesn't care about whether it's his idea or who had the idea first," said Adam Virant, one of our coaches. "His mind moves in a certain way. His goal is to always make it provocative, different, and super memorable. He believes in letting smart people do their thing. You don't see him one-upping people. But he will lead you down a path or take the reins on ideas if it's stalling. He brings you back to home base: Why are we here? What do we stand for? The process is stimulating."

Even when we're not in Monday OTT mode, it's still open season on ideas.

I might roll into the locker room on game day and randomly ask, "Anybody got any crazy ideas?" Our players are eager to respond. The crazier the idea, the better. Sometimes, I'll latch on to an idea immediately, and fans will see it pop up in the third inning.

Once we have the idea, it's all about execution. Most often, we will rehearse it meticulously, sometimes a few hours before game time. It's the old *Saturday Night Live* model that Lorne Michaels uses. On the set, *SNL* actors throw ideas and improvisation around freely, but once the troupe hones in on an idea, it goes to work on ensuring the timing is precise.

I consider the WWE as the gold standard in sports entertainment. They have frequent performances in front of a live crowd and a television audience, usually two to three times a week. It's year-round storytelling.

It's different from any other sports league because they all go dormant for several months during their off-season. There's nothing going on. And as I see it, when you're not playing, you're losing fans. That happened for a lot of teams in 2020 during COVID.

The WWE has a successful model the same way Jeff Bezos does with Amazon. If you look back at Amazon, everything is about clicking on that model. Lower prices drive a better customer experience. A better customer experience drives more customers, which then drives more sellers onto the website. And that continues to lower the cost because of the competition, which then drives more customers.

The Bananas also have a model. It starts with live events. Those live events drive more content. More content drives more traffic. More traffic drives more demand for live events. So we keep coming up with more ideas to drive more content to produce more fans who create the demand for more live events. It never stops.

We also have a creative model that starts with what I call our

PCPs. That stands for performer, creator, and producer. Some-one who performs on the field will create content and also produce it. The more PCPs we have, the more ideas we can generate. More ideas will drive more content. And more content will attract more PCPs.

The reality is we have our players: Princess Potassia, our break-dancing first-base coach, our umpire, all these people who perform in our live events. They create content, and they also produce it. They're all working our model constantly. The MLB, NBA, NFL, and NHL have nothing like that. I get it. Their model doesn't allow for it.

The WWE comes closest to that model concept. But I think our show is dramatically different. If I got to a game early, I'd hope for something more than a rerun of a movie. But when I went to a WWE show, it had zero live events before the show. They played three movies. We make sure that's not going to hap-pen. In our pregame, there are sometimes fifty promotions. We move really fast and give fans plenty to watch and enjoy.

During our World Tour, fans with VIP passes joined us on the field during pregame and watched us rehearse our routines, which can include dances or other gags. And there's an impor-tant distinction to make because new fans to the Bananas some-times get confused: we rehearse our dances and comedy routines, but the baseball itself is not staged or rehearsed.

The competition between the Bananas and Party Animals is 100 percent authentic.

When a bunch of men held a bachelor party at a Bananas game, they were convinced it was fake and bet on the Bananas. They were shocked to see the Party Animals prevail and, from what I understand, lost a bundle.

Now, even the Party Animals have developed their own rooting section in each city. There's even a demand now for Party Animals gear.

When we first picked out players at the World Tour tryouts, we next worked to divide them as evenly as possible. So who became a Banana and who became a Party Animal?

Like the professional wrestling model, the Bananas are the good guys, the heroes who are "America's team." The Party Animals are the heels, the villains who feed off the boos.

"Hey, we need a little love, too, but we'll never get as much as the Bananas do," said catcher Mike Vavasis, who was one of our Party Animal stalwarts in 2022. "We're the Bananas with no filter, the grimy Bananas. I do have to explain it to people. They think we're there for comedy relief or to be the fall guys. No, not exactly. Not only are the games not fixed, but we're out there for blood. We love to entertain. But you better believe this, too: we hate to lose."

The Bananas and Party Animals exist in the same orbit and even ride the same bus on the road. But when the games are done and you visit the losing side, it's like the World Series has just been decided. Each game is bragging rights on steroids. That level of competitiveness—along with our entertainment—gives us the complete package.

There are some things in baseball that can't be faked. You can either hit a ninety-four-mile-an-hour fastball or you can't. You can either go deep in the hole at shortstop to throw a guy out or you can't. I'm confident that anybody who watches Bananas games, night in and night out, will come away impressed with the competition and the skill level.

"The Savannah Bananas? Oh yeah, they're the Harlem Globetrotters of baseball."

I take that as a compliment, although I don't believe it's entirely accurate.

Most every sports fan has heard about the Globetrotters, the masters of fancy dribbling, trick shots, and crowd-pleasing antics. Like many kids, I grew up watching Meadowlark Lemon, Curly Neal, and all those other incredible basketball showmen who warmed up to "Sweet Georgia Brown."

We've seen them hide the ball under their jerseys or do the weave or make like they were throwing a bucket of water into the crowd, only to find out it was a bunch of confetti.

The Globetrotters have been around since 1926, and they have performed in 123 countries. No doubt, they have taken their act to an arena near you.

But did you realize that the Harlem Globetrotters are a big reason for the growth and popularity of the NBA? It's true. In 1948 and 1949, the barnstorming Globetrotters twice defeated the all-white Minneapolis Lakers, who were champions of the NBA. For years, the Globetrotters had been booked on the front end of doubleheaders by NBA owners, who were desperate to attract larger crowds.

Because of the Globetrotters, and the belief that they were the world's best basketball team, the NBA integrated and signed their first Black player in 1950. They took a regional, small-time sport and helped propel it on the path to become an internationally known product with some of the world's most famous athletes.

The Globetrotters went in another direction. They kept delivering the incredible ballhandling, rim-rattling dunks, and unforgettable comedy routines, but the games weren't flat-out competition.

They still perform about four hundred live events per year.

But their main opponent, the Washington Generals, weren't really there to win. The Generals became one of sports' all-time losers, snapping a 2,495-game losing streak in 1971 essentially because the Globetrotters got so caught up in the entertainment that they lost track of the score.

During decades of touring, the Globetrotters have been on the wrong end of the final score less than 0.2 percent of the time. That was always by design and was a huge part of the show. These days, people still love the same Globetrotter gags and schtick that I enjoyed as a kid.

That is *not* the Savannah Bananas.

Except for a few dance numbers and our "Hey Baby" routine with the crowd in the fourth inning, we don't stage anything. We do not know who's going to win. And we are constantly changing our promotions and routines, night after night. It's not true to say if a person has seen one Bananas game they have seen them all. We are different every night. And the baseball game itself is definitely different.

To our players, the mere thought of trying to stage a baseball game is folly.

"The Globetrotters are insanely fun and probably really good for the sport of basketball, just like I think we're really good for baseball," said Kyle Luigs, one of our pitchers. "But we can't script out a baseball game, no matter how hard we try. It would be absurdly obvious. Whoever wins is going to win. The Party Animals are not only allowed to win, but they're just as talented, if not more talented, than we are. It's competition and there are some harsh words exchanged at times."

"In basketball, you can let somebody have a free lane and get a dunk . . . and I guess you can miss shots on purpose," said Michael Deeb, one of our outfielders. "In baseball, you can't fake it.

Even with all the entertainment aspects, it's baseball. It's not a clown show. It's legit stuff—with all the entertainment wrinkles—and you've got to be able to play this game well to even make the Bananas team."

We may be different, but I deeply respect what the Globetrotters did and how they fundamentally changed the game of basketball. They traveled everywhere and took the hard road to figure out how to keep playing games and how to stay afloat.

And they discovered that even as great as their basketball abilities were, their entertainment skills were the answer. Some of it happened by mistake. As the story goes, the Globetrotters were playing in a freezing-cold gymnasium in Minnesota and using the fire of a stove burner to keep the place warm. When one of the players got pushed out of bounds, he landed in the coals. His backside caught on fire, causing him to run around in a panic. The whole crowd laughed hysterically, thinking it was part of the act.

Abe Saperstein, their founder, saw that and said, "Hey, there's something there."

It wasn't just basketball. Entertainment made the Globetrotters different. I think the Savannah Bananas realized that concept right away, and that's how we've built our baseball show.

Fundamentally, I want the Bananas to have the same impact on baseball that the Globetrotters had on basketball. We're hoping to be even more long-lasting and sustainable, although the Globetrotters have essentially been around for a century.

But I'd rather not be known as the Globetrotters of baseball. When someone thinks of creative, fun things, I want people to say it's the Savannah Bananas of this or the Savannah Bananas of that. In time, as our brand grows, I definitely feel we will become that kind of reference point. Because even though when fans compare the Bananas to the Globetrotters, in most senses, it's a compliment, I struggle with the comparison.

Before the COVID pandemic, we took our whole staff to the Globetrotters show when they came to Savannah. Unfortunately, it bored us because it was geared toward a younger fan base. Their show is also the same every single place they go. It's nearly identical to the one I watched as a child.

I think people recognize that the Bananas and Globetrotters both try to have fun, so I know where people are coming from when they make the comparison. And if anything, with the challenges of staying relevant and finding bigger and bigger audiences, that's where my mind is focused.

How do we get there?

Ideas, ideas, and more ideas.

"My son was a big TikTok follower of the Bananas before I got my audition," said Vincent Chapman, our dancing home-plate umpire, when he was interviewed for this book. "You watch it there and certainly appreciate it. But until you are actually involved, you have no idea what it takes to pull this off. I'm not sure Jesse's brain ever stops or he ever sleeps. The Bananas are thinking two or three years down the line."

"I see a ton of moving parts, a ton of logistics, and that could be overwhelming, but the Bananas are never going to stop innovating," said Jake Peavy, the pitcher who was a World Series champion and a Cy Young Award winner. "The Bananas seem to have that down. They are really not afraid to try something new."

Jake knows that better than anyone. In 2021, when we strayed from our Savannah home base for the first time to play Banana Ball in the great city of Mobile, Alabama, we called it a One-City World Tour and sold out both nights.

Was it all completely perfect? Nope. Just like anyone would

expect on the first night at a new stadium. Our national anthem singer got stuck in traffic, so we had the fans sing together for a patriotic moment. We did a tribute to Hank Aaron, one of Mobile's fabled baseball products, but the audio messed up and no one could hear anything I said.

But by the second night's game, which the Bananas won on a walk-off in the showdown, it all seemed perfect. I grabbed the microphone and said, "Mobile, you've been great! We love you guys so much! Now we've got one more surprise for you."

Boom. Lights off.

Surprise fireworks show.

At that moment, we started playing a medley from *The Greatest Showman* soundtrack. The place went nuts. One of our team members saw a woman holding her two kids and tears were coming down her face. That's why we do this entertainment. It means everything to see people have emotional reactions and enjoy themselves so much.

I knew we had nailed it, and I knew that touring from city to city would be our future. I ran through the concourse, feeling like I had just won the World Series, probably looking like a kid in the world's biggest candy store. I ran up to our band because I wanted to be there with them so I could greet every single fan leaving the game.

But our band members were exhausted. They had been playing for forty-five minutes. Most of them had put their instruments down for a rest while the drummer did a solo. Sean McBride, the bandleader, told me they just needed a breather and they would finish strong.

All of a sudden, I heard our tuba player doing the opening beat to "Stand by Me."

There were maybe four hundred people still outside. Both

teams were there, greeting everyone. But when that song started, our players and staff came in, then put their arms around one another. Then the fans joined in: every type of person in that baseball experience and they're all arm in arm, swaying and singing to "Stand by Me."

That was not planned.

But now it's our closing tradition.

I get goose bumps every time I think about it. Sometimes, the best ideas just kind of happen.

Chapter Eighteen

2022 World Tour

We couldn't have picked a more amazing venue to finish our 2022 World Tour. We were in Birmingham, Alabama—at Rickwood Field, the oldest surviving ballpark in America. Banana Ball was going to breathe some life back into the beautiful old place.

We had had some sticky situations at our other stops—Daytona Beach, Florida; Montgomery, Alabama; West Palm Beach, Florida; and Columbus, Georgia—but nothing like this. A few hours before Birmingham game time, we were in big, big trouble.

We were expecting the biggest crowd in Rickwood Field history—ten thousand—but every time I checked my phone's weather radar, it showed a huge green cell coming right for us. Chance of rain: 100 percent.

We were scrambling. Our game was set for five o'clock and Rickwood's lights didn't work. Even if the rain stopped, how could we get the game in before dark? This was our one shot. The next day was Easter Sunday. That wasn't a good replacement date because everyone wanted to get home and be with their families.

Rickwood, which opened in 1910, had seen better days. Its

sound system didn't work, so we brought our own. The concessions were in tents outside the stadium. Miraculously, there was a tarp and we had it on the field. It was starting to sprinkle when we gathered the players around.

"Would you be willing to play in the pouring rain?"

We weren't forcing anyone to risk injury, but we didn't want to disappoint the ten thousand Banana Ball fans, either.

We had to try to play this game.

Then the most amazing thing happened: it didn't rain. I guess that green cell took one look at Banana Ball, didn't want to mess with us, and turned around.

We played the game—and what a game it was!

This game featured Jake Peavy and Bill Lee as the pitchers. That's right. Our old friend Jake Peavy, the former Cy Young winner, gave us a strong inning, and he used his actual Gold Glove, which Rawlings had provided with his award. Bill Lee, seventy-five years young, warmed up with his grandsons Ethan and Brandon Burkes in the bullpen. Then he performed well in the game, giving the fans a thrill.

Our director of entertainment, Zack Frongillo, came up to the plate after displaying his ballet skill with spins, turnouts, and pirouettes . . . then got a hit. And we had the most theatrical ending anyone could have imagined—our head coach, Eric Byrnes, sent himself up as a pinch hitter with the tying run on third base. With the sellout crowd on its feet and roaring, Byrnesie got hooked on a strike-three call, and the Bananas lost by one to the Party Animals.

It was still pretty darn perfect.

Hundreds of fans came on the field to meet our players, and nobody wanted to leave. Honestly, I didn't want to leave, either. Our World Tour was a huge success and it proved our hope once and for all: Banana Ball could not only work outside of Savannah; it could thrive.

When we put together our World Tour, there were dozens of things that could have gone wrong. I'm sure when restaurants open their first out-of-town location, the management wonders, *Hey, will this work in a different city?*

We were confident that Banana Ball would be received well. But we wanted to give ourselves the best chance at success. We selected each city for a specific reason. Each one was an intentional experiment.

Could we work with a major-league spring training stadium? How about minor-league stadiums of different shapes and sizes? If we went to a smaller city for a midweek game, would we still draw enough fans? Would it have the same level of enthusiasm as on the weekend? Could we move our team and our people efficiently from city to city? What about the hotels? What about the food?

It's one thing to do this successfully in Savannah—and of course we worked our homesite into the tour on two weekends. Our players and staff could sleep in their own beds. They did laundry at their own houses. They appreciated things that made life easier—groceries, taking care of pets, sticking to a routine— because the road can be a grind.

But we wanted Banana Ball to grow. Our goal is to play before one million people by 2025 and many, many more by 2030, maybe sooner. So we have to prepare by experimenting. We want to know what works and what doesn't.

When the teams arrive at a city for one game and it gets rained out, it disappoints the fans who counted on seeing Banana Ball. At some of our sites, we had fans attending from more than thirty different states. I struggle with things like that. I try to control everything I possibly can, but some things I have to trust and let go.

We were followed at every stop by an ESPN crew, which was shooting footage for *Bananaland,* a five-part documentary that told our story in such an awesome way and gave us outstanding exposure. I was constantly miked up, and I don't think the crew missed documenting anything. We gave them free rein. I think they shot about three hundred hours' worth of action, then somehow got it boiled down to five hours.

Daytona Beach was our first stop in 2022 and really the first time we went into another market with an existing minor-league team. If a market is saturated with sports, there could be a potential risk. But there were enough fans within a two-hour radius of the city that ticket sales weren't a problem.

Then there are the logistical issues with every ballpark. In the older ones, like Jackie Robinson Stadium in Daytona Beach, there are small concourses, so it can be challenging to get the flow of foot traffic going a certain way. We do things differently from minor-league teams because our fans line up an hour or so beforehand and get entertained outside of the stadium. The normal traffic patterns do not apply. We had problems with the sound system, which lost its volume on the first night. The first night is always stressful. By the second night, there's a functional plan.

At Daytona, thousands of fans milled about just beyond the outfield wall, stretching from foul pole to foul pole, in anticipation of the gates opening. It was individual fans, families, groups of teens, grandparents with kids, high school players. They were in line, waiting for Banana Ball to begin. The sound of that—the buzz of the fans anticipating all the fun—never gets old, and it makes every night feel like it's the first time we ever did this.

I tell our staff to look for that one fan, that one opportunity to make a difference. When you have four thousand people in the stands, it looks like a blur of yellow. But there's always that one fan. What that means is we give special treatment to every fan.

One of our game hosts, Tyler Gray, always looks for someone who's sitting by themselves. Then we create a special fuss over that person. On this night, he found a woman who was supposed to attend the game with her daughter. But she came alone when her daughter got held up at work. It turned out she had lost her father just before Christmas; then her best friend had died of cancer the week before. When her daughter couldn't come to the game, she was down in the dumps and was sitting in a row all by herself.

Tyler, who was wearing his leopard-skin jacket, asked the crowd to show her some love. Tyler then gave her a full-body hug. As she told me later, "My sad thoughts were replaced with awesomeness. I played a part in the Greatest Show on Earth."

The game itself was tremendous. By the end of the two-hour time limit, the Bananas and Party Animals were tied. Then the teams went through three rounds of the showdown—the batter against just the pitcher, catcher, and one defender on the infield—before Michael Deeb won it for the Bananas on an RBI single.

And that was the best ending of all.

Michael put smiles on everyone's faces before the game, too. When a young fan asked Michael for an autograph, he agreed, but only if the fan would give him his autograph, too. The fan happily accommodated Michael, as did some of his friends, and when Michael smacked that game-winning RBI single, he did it wearing a jersey and cap filled with young fans' signatures.

Although we didn't know it at the time, Jackie Robinson Stadium has consistently given good karma to Michael Deeb. After the game, he told us that when he was ten, he had played in a tennis tournament at Daytona Beach. Then he saw his first college baseball game—at Jackie Robinson Stadium. In the third grade, Michael wrote a paper on Jackie Robinson, then later wore number 42 as a Notre Dame football player in his honor. He became a graduate transfer baseball player at Bethune-Cookman University, where the team played at . . . Jackie Robinson Stadium.

The night before our first Banana Ball game in Daytona Beach, Michael hopped the fence at Jackie Robinson Stadium in the pitch-black dark and found his way to the plate, where he visualized hitting a home run and then took a lap around the bases. Of course, he became the game's hero.

"Too many stars were aligned," Michael said.

One of the delighted adult fans was Colby Kortis from Orlando, who found us on TikTok. He wondered why baseball players were wearing kilts and said he needed to know more. Colby said he had been to twenty-six major-league games in ten different ballparks the previous year, but he had never seen anything like Banana Ball.

"We never stopped moving and dancing, and we saw so many crazy plays that the baseball old fogies might not like," Colby said. "My God, that was a great freaking game. Can they all be like that?"

A few weekends later, we played in West Palm Beach at the Ballpark of the Palm Beaches, where the Houston Astros and Washington Nationals share a spring training home. It's a beautiful ballpark with some of the softest, greenest grass anyone could ever see. It was like the Bananas had made it to Broadway.

Spring training games are primarily played during the day, so we were assigned the Friday night game. We quickly sold that one out—more than seven thousand tickets. That must have gotten someone's attention because we were supposed to play on Saturday night, too, but they moved us to Saturday afternoon and put the spring training game at night.

The Astros played the Miami Marlins on that Friday afternoon. The game drew about one thousand fans and thankfully they got it done in about two and a half hours, so we had enough time to do our normal show. When Marlins manager Don Mattingly left, he spotted our head coach, Eric Byrnes, whom he knew from the big leagues.

"Byrnsie? What are you doing here?"

"I'm coaching the Bananas."

Mattingly just shook his head. "Of course you are. That makes all the sense in the world."

We heard from fans that tickets to our Bananas game went for hundreds of dollars on the secondary market. And we put on a great performance. Those seven thousand fans were active and involved like never before. Christian Dearman's grandparents Bill and Sue danced on top of our dugout to celebrate more than sixty years of marriage. One of the ushers said he had never seen a more revved-up crowd in that stadium.

By the end of the night, everyone's energy was expended. After we did our "Stand by Me" rendition on the plaza and went out arm in arm with the fans—everyone together, Bananas, Party Animals, staff members—some of our pep band members were lying down, exhausted. They had truly given it everything.

The next morning, while our players took batting practice on the back fields, an Astros assistant coach approached Adam Virant, one of our coaches.

"He said he was immersed in the craziness of it all . . . and he wished the game lasted two more hours," Viro said. "And this was a grizzled veteran coach, a baseball lifer. He thought Banana Ball was awesome."

We had more surprises in the second game. Johnny Bench, maybe the greatest catcher of all time, was our first-base coach. Johnny lives in the area, and when he heard the Bananas were coming, he wanted to be a part of it. We were happy to oblige and showed him some Bananas hospitality.

"Johnny, we're so thrilled that you're here," I told him.

"Are you kidding? I love the Bananas," Johnny said. "I think what you guys are doing is absolutely fantastic. I'm thrilled to be part of it."

Of course Johnny took the credit when Dakota McFadden popped a home run in the first inning. Johnny was hamming it up; then he noticed Dakota standing in the dugout after rounding the bases. He called Dakota out for a big hug, and the crowd roared again.

"The Bananas may set the standard for all of baseball," Johnny said later. "What they're doing is revolutionary. Such passion and love for the game. We all want to be entertained. I'm not sure we'll see Max Scherzer doing the tango or a flip, but this will catch on. When people go to Bananas games, it's like returning to their childhood, when baseball was more simple. That's why it works so well."

We had been anxious about how things would work in a major-league spring training stadium. But we'd barely left West Palm Beach, still giddy about how well it had gone, when we got a call from the stadium operations manager there: "What will it take to get you guys back?"

That was great to hear, but I can't pretend that everything worked well throughout the tour. We learned plenty. Numerous things were off-kilter in Montgomery. We were forced to change a lot of the promotional script, but it's good to learn how to think on your feet like that. The stadium ran out of popcorn and pretzels because it hadn't counted on so many fans. Compared to that, Columbus was a disaster. The stadium didn't have enough food. Fans were told it would be an hour wait for pizza—and they still never got it. We can control only so much in some of the cities. We double-check and triple-check. Still, things go wrong. That's part of the risk of taking the games out of Savannah. But we learned some valuable lessons. We hope mistakes won't be repeated.

Of all the stadiums we visited, Birmingham's had the fewest amenities. The bank of lights—added in 1936—didn't even function. But the Rickwood Field staff was organized and determined. It became our best experience of the World Tour.

Man, what a place. I felt transported back to another time. I probably should've shown up in a suit and top hat, maybe smoking a cigar, even though I don't smoke. During Rickwood's heyday, that's the way it was. Fans showed up in their Sunday best and enjoyed the ballgame.

Babe Ruth, Ty Cobb, Ted Williams, Stan Musial, and Reggie Jackson played at Rickwood. So did a sixteen-year-old rookie named Willie Mays. They still talk about the Negro league battles between Satchel Paige of the Black Barons and the likes of Josh Gibson and Cool Papa Bell. Rickwood is where 42—the movie about Jackie Robinson—was filmed.

Minor-league baseball left the heart of Birmingham after

1987, first for the suburbs, then for a sparkling new $64 million stadium in the city.

Rickwood Field was all but forgotten on the professional circuit. It has continued to host high school games and amateur tournaments, along with the Rickwood Classic vintage game, held each year since 1996, when the minor-league Barons return to play against a Southern League opponent. But things were never the same. The Friends of Rickwood group battled not only to keep the stadium open but also to prevent it from being torn down.

We were fired up to play at such a cool setting. But between all the extra preparations and the ominous weather, our Birmingham game day was a roller coaster in every way. There were moments when we weren't sure if we could play. We got lucky with the rain. Maybe it was destiny, because I feel like Banana Ball brought the place to life.

It really hit me during the national anthem when I looked around at ten thousand fans in that classic setting. I won't forget that moment.

Right after the game, I was thinking about details and capping the experience for the fans. I'm not sure I immediately grasped the enormity of what Banana Ball meant for Rickwood Field.

Gerald Watkins, chairman of the board and chief executive officer of Rickwood Field, said he and his staff had tears in their eyes.

"It was fabulous . . . way beyond expectations," Gerald said. "So many people came to our park today for the first time. Now they'll think about Rickwood Field and come back, maybe bring a Little League team, maybe donate money.

"We had a nice crowd in 2010 for our one-hundredth anniversary, but nothing like this. This was jam, jam, jam-packed. I saw so much happiness in the faces of people. I saw people who were so happy to be here, even though there were long lines. So many kids were here. Memories were made. This provided such hope for our old ballpark. The whole thing was off the charts. The Bananas provided us pure joy, and I think with what they're doing, it's going to make a whole new generation of fans love baseball."

Before the World Tour started, I told the players I wanted it to be the most fun they had ever had playing baseball. And I think we lived up to that. Wherever they go in life, I hope they bring the Bananas with them. I hope they bring some fun. I hope they remember what "Fans First" is all about. I hope they remember how they made a kid feel and how they high-fived the fans before and after the game. I hope they remember all of that, because that's what's going to make baseball work in the future.

The Bananas are all about a new way to play baseball. But we have such respect for the game's history and these grand old ballparks. To think that we can tie together the generations like that, it's pretty overwhelming.

When we had tryouts and picked the Bananas and Party Animals, we didn't know what was ahead. We had no idea. We knew the fans were excited. We hoped every game would be competitive and entertaining—and we arranged the teams with that goal in mind. We certainly didn't know how it would work in older ballparks, or whether we could even put on our kind of show. There were tremendous challenges, but it worked. The Bananas brought life into a storied ballpark that had been dormant, and for us, it was incredibly special. Watching the fans come together and giving them a taste of another time meant the world to our organization.

Chapter Nineteen

Kansas City, Here We Come!

We already knew how Banana Ball worked in Savannah. The World Tour proved to us that it could work anywhere. We wondered if people would respond. It was equal parts chaos, sideshow, and baseball, so I think it had something for everyone. And to see the energy go several levels beyond in each of these very diverse stadiums, it was definitely real.

After Birmingham, we had a break of about three weeks. Some of our guys moved on to independent league teams, so there were emotional farewells.

Our biggest challenge was still ahead: the chance to play a two-game series against the Kansas City Monarchs, an excellent independent league team filled with former major leaguers. Could Banana Ball stand up to that challenge? We were about to find out.

We came into this with some trepidation. Did the Bananas belong with the Kansas City Monarchs? Could the Monarchs adapt to our Banana Ball rules? Could we transport all of our players and cast members on a plane, then deliver an efficient show to meet everyone's expectations?

The answers: yes, yes, yes!

When our two-game set with the Monarchs was done, deep into the Kansas City night, I was dancing.

Man, I was dancing. I've never danced harder. I've never danced longer. Since we started the Savannah Bananas, after nearly every game, my mind had always been racing. What was next? What can we learn? What can we do better?

I'm an emotional guy. And I'm not the kind of guy who takes a breath, either. It's go, go, go. But there I was, completely lost in the moment. They were playing "Cupid Shuffle," the players and hundreds of fans were dancing together, and I just wanted the sheer happiness to last forever.

The same thought kept racing through my head:

We did this!

We did this!

We did this!

Look, I was a little scared when we accepted a two-game challenge from the Monarchs. I was also extremely intrigued by the whole idea. The Monarchs were the original barnstorming team in the Negro leagues. Those who played for the Monarchs are legendary: Buck O'Neil. Cool Papa Bell. Satchel Paige. Jackie Robinson.

Now the Monarchs are an independent league team, a really good one that has won the American Association title. They had eight guys who had played in the major leagues, including a handful who'd played in the bigs the previous season. With that level of competition, the outside observers and the naysayers had the same question. Were we crazy?

Well, maybe. Hey, we all have got to be a little bit crazy sometimes. Everyone's got to experiment. Everyone's got to push themselves out of their comfort zones. Some people thought we were bananas to try such a thing. But what do you expect from the Bananas? It's what we do.

One way or another, we were going to answer some really important questions to define the Bananas' future:

Could we compete against MLB-level players?

Could another team, maybe even a hardened, skeptical team, agree to our Banana Ball rules, let their traditional baseball guard down, and enjoy our brand of fans-first fun and entertainment?

Could we efficiently move more than one hundred players and cast members—by plane, for the first time—along with a Penske truckload of our merchandise, supplies, and props for a journey one thousand miles from our home base?

We did it all. The Monarchs agreed to Banana Ball rules— 100 percent. They were great about it and picked it up quickly. We did it all really well. And the Kansas City weekend took our dreams from theory to reality. We can go to Texas. We can go to California. One day, we'll probably go overseas. Banana Ball in the shadow of the Eiffel Tower? Somewhere in Asia? Australia? Why not? It's all on the table now.

The Kansas City trip put into practice so many of our core values. Being bold. Believing in our brand. Experimenting. Getting better.

When we planned the tour, we based it on expanding our reach but still focusing on the Southeast. We looked at going to Florida, another part of Georgia, and to a couple of cities in Alabama. The tour would be held in the same general area. It would just be a longer bus ride.

Kansas City was a completely different venture.

I give credit to Mark McKee, the Monarchs' CEO. He pursued us. He grasped what the Bananas were doing and saw benefits—both financial and in terms of exposure for his club.

At first, the timing wasn't great. We would have to take a break of several weeks before playing in Kansas City. Some of our players would be unavailable due to their commitments to independent league teams of their own. In all the other cities, we were playing our own team—the Bananas against the Party Animals—not an outside opponent. I knew we'd have to fly to Kansas City, so the expenses would be high.

Sensing my hesitation, Mark offered to help fund the Bananas' travel, and we discussed how we could work together to make it happen. Mark's proposal took care of meals, and it gave us a special deal on the hotel along with a generous sum of money on top of that to help cover costs. What did we have to lose? Our staff flew over to check out their stadium, Legends Field, and decided that it would be a really good test for the Bananas.

We were playing a quality opponent in a different region of the country. If it worked, we could exponentially grow to new markets and expose thousands upon thousands of new fans to Banana Ball. That was certainly worth a shot.

When all the tickets for Kansas City sold in just sixteen minutes, it solidified our decision. We would draw fans from thirty-two states, and we were motivated to put on a great show.

Being part of the Kansas City Monarchs and their barnstorming tradition meant the world to me. But that really hit home when we got to Kansas City and took our team and staff to the Negro Leagues Baseball Museum. Bob Kendrick, the museum president, gave us a private tour; there were about fifty of us in all—me and Emily, our staff, and some of our players.

We stood at silent attention as Bob, a gifted speaker, explained to us that American historians in the past never viewed the Negro leagues as truly professional. "If you don't control the pen," he said, "you don't control the story," meaning so much of the Negro leagues story went unnoticed. All these years later, the museum is dedicated to telling that story with accuracy and relevance.

"They wouldn't let them in the major leagues, so they started their own league," Bob said. "That's the American spirit. Won't let me play with you? Well, I'm gonna create my own league."

Wow, that really hit home.

One of our pitchers, Mat Wolf, got emotional, too. Mat's the guy with all the trick pitches—behind his back, through his legs, cartwheeling, spinning, his hat going one way, the ball another way. He calls one of his twenty-four pitches "Satchel to Satchel," and another is named for Goose Tatum, one of the original clown princes who later took his dramatic moves on the road with the basketball Globetrotters. Mat stood transfixed as he watched a black-and-white Goose Tatum video. He had watched it dozens of times before while teaching himself Goose's flamboyant style of pitching. It was as if Mat realized that his passion was shared by so much of the baseball world and he was just discovering the full impact of his hero.

When Bob compared the Bananas to the Indianapolis Clowns, it was a very emotional validation. The Clowns were known as a barnstorming sideshow and their antics were the inspiration for the 1976 film *The Bingo Long Traveling All-Stars & Motor Kings*. We're also after high-level showmanship and entertainment.

"The Clowns brought that same kind of entertainment," Bob said. "People saw Richard 'King Tut' King with his oversized glove, Goose Tatum, the three-feet, two-inch Ralph 'Spec Bebop' Bell, and they never forgot that. Because it was an experience. People won't forget the Bananas, either, because they are an experience.

"When you went to a Negro league game, you were thoroughly

entertained. The style was bold, aggressive, and daring. You didn't know what zany thing or interaction was coming next. It was great fundamental baseball, but you were also giving them a show. Buck O'Neil always said you couldn't go to the concession stand because you might miss something that had never been seen before. Y'all ever heard that with the Bananas?"

Bob's speech helped focus our determination to bring our best show to Kansas City. Still, my fear wouldn't go away. Walt Disney always talked about controlling the controllables. We were surrendering part of that control by playing another team. When we're playing the Party Animals, the entertainment is timed out and carefully staged. We were stepping into a bit of the unknown.

I'm obsessed and fanatical about our show because I'm such a perfectionist. It was scary to think that more than thirteen thousand fans were coming from around the country over two nights to watch Banana Ball . . . and half of what happens on the field is *being executed by a team that is not accustomed to Banana Ball.*

I knew we would put on a good show. But could the Monarchs play a part in that and do it well? This was their first crack at Banana Ball and the rules are different.

A few days before, one of our coaches, Adam Virant (Viro); our entertainment director, Zack Frongillo; and some members of the Monarchs staff discussed the mechanics of the game on a Zoom call. We didn't know how the Monarchs were preparing. We needed to explain Banana Ball to the host team so they would be ready for our unique showmanship.

Since the agreement was that the two teams would play Banana Ball rules, Viro and Zack assumed the manager and players who were on the call would have been excited and optimistic about the event. Instead, the Monarchs came off as less than enthused on the call, so much that Viro tried to lighten the mood by throwing out a joke: "OK, how bad do you guys hate this?" Still, the hosts had no reaction. Finally, the manager conceded that the rules sounded good, but he still wasn't happy with the two-hour time limit on the games.

Later, I learned that the team's owner hadn't told the manager the Monarchs would be playing Banana Ball until the last minute. The manager's focus was on starting spring training and getting the season underway. He had planned on using players from their backup team (consisting of players who competed at lower levels) because he thought the two-game event would be more of a scrimmage than a competition. The owner, though, insisted that the manager play his top players, a decision that left the manager less than thrilled.

When our team arrived at the field on Friday, I was still pretty uneasy about the whole thing. We gathered for our normal pregame meeting with the players, but the Monarchs were there, too, to go through the routine of the promotions. As Viro went through the rules and told them what to expect, a few of them started smiling and laughing. "Oh, hell yeah, this will be good." When we taught them the "Hey Baby" dance, the smiles got bigger.

It was so cool to see the Monarchs high-fiving people, signing autographs, really into it. When we did our pregame wrestling-style weigh-in at home plate, a bit of mirth and silliness that makes you laugh despite its odd position in a baseball game, they sent out Matt Adams. They call him "Big City" because he comes in at 260 pounds. This guy is a super-legit ballplayer. Matt played ten years in the big leagues and hit twenty homers for the Washington Nationals during their 2019 World Series run. Previously, he had played for the Colorado Rockies.

Matt Adams came to the weigh-in with one of those giant WWE belts. He was hamming it up. He got with our weigh-in guy, Collin Ledbetter, and they did a combo dance, then played patty-cake. It was hilarious. The "weigh-in" actually has no relevance to the baseball game at all. It's more of a funny visual. Baseball players might be wondering, *What the heck is this nonsense?* But Matt Adams played along, and the crowd loved it. So I was thinking, *OK, a few of their leaders have the spirit. This might work.*

As for the Bananas, we had not played or practiced in nearly three weeks. We didn't have our shortstop, Ryan Cox, or any of our regular outfielders, Jake Skole, Reece Hampton, and Dakota McFadden, because they had reported to their independent league pro teams. We added some Party Animals to round out the full Bananas team, and we also brought in former major-leaguer Jonny Gomes, a big fan favorite because he had been part of the Kansas City Royals team that won a World Series in 2015—but we were going in severely short on our regular talent.

I don't usually think about the baseball game because that takes care of itself, but this time I had concerns, and my fears came to life.

We were the home team even though it was the Monarchs' field, so they batted first. Right from the start, the Monarchs scored six runs in the first inning. Our defense played sloppily and made errors on the first two plays. Our catcher, Bill LeRoy, left the game after a pitch bounced and caromed under his mask and hit him in the neck. He was disoriented and couldn't catch his breath. We hadn't had any injuries during the whole tour, but after Bill left the game in the first inning, two other players got hurt and left the game later. When we finally got up, our first batter, Chris Vazquez, took two strikes, then fouled one back into the crowd, and a fan caught it. In Banana Ball, that's an out. Even our own rules were conspiring against us.

It was painful to watch. We hadn't allowed six runs in an inning the entire tour, but this game—the first one where we intended to prove we belonged—we gave up six runs early. Although you never can tell what will happen with baseball, I honestly felt embarrassed.

My dad had come from his Massachusetts home, just as he did for many of our Banana Ball games. I looked him in the eyes a few times and muttered to myself, "This isn't how we drew it up." I was in the dugout feeling very frustrated. Once we escaped that inning, things improved. Because of the Banana Ball rules, that six-run inning actually was worth just one point for the Monarchs, so the damage wasn't that bad.

The Monarchs let their starters go through the lineup; then they started substituting liberally with players from their backup team. Most of them were former pro players and some were older. These were not household names by any means.

Still, we fought and scratched and found ourselves trailing just 3–2 going into the last inning. With two outs, we put a runner on base, and if we could just get him home, we'd go to the showdown tiebreaker, an improbability considering how poorly we'd played at the game's outset. Dalton Cornett fouled one back and it was caught by a fan—again—and that should've been the final out.

But when our umpire, Vincent Chapman, went over to investigate, the surrounding fans claimed the ball hadn't been caught. Our ump took them at their word. It didn't matter. Dalton froze on a 3–2 backdoor slider and it was over on a called strike three.

Monarchs 3, Bananas 2. It didn't sound bad at all. Everybody had a great time, including the Monarchs. I thought we came back as well as possible from a brutal first inning. It was embarrassing to start, but our team was all-in on the show. Hopefully the baseball followed suit.

I can't use my mental bandwidth to worry about the actual baseball and other things I can't control. It's not a good use of my mental space. So even though the six thousand or so fans had had a great time, I slept maybe two hours that night. I went into the hotel bathroom so I wouldn't wake up Emily and the kids, and started making notes of script ideas and enhancements.

This is the way I think: *Can we create better content and attract more fans that way? If we didn't play well again in the second game, could we make it an even better show?*

At three in the morning, I was still making my script enhancements. I didn't realize that down the hall in another hotel room, Christian Dearman, who would start the next game, couldn't sleep, either. He was fired up.

I found out later that after the game, the Bananas had had a verbal run-in with the Monarchs' clubhouse attendant.

As Christian, first baseman Dan Oberst, and our evening's pitcher, Kyle Luigs walked past the Monarchs' clubhouse on their way to the postgame meal, the clubhouse attendant kind of smirked at them and said, "You guys weren't expecting us to beat you, huh?"

As the trio of Bananas looked at one another in disbelief, the clubbie kept talking. He said the Monarchs had had to put in their backup players so the game could stay close and they'd probably need to do that again on Saturday. "Yeah, we have some real pro players here," he said.

In addition to the clubhouse attendant's comments, Christian also had heard some Monarch fans refer to the Bananas as a "joke" or "fake pros" during our rough first inning. Christian was now like a man possessed.

"I am always up for a challenge and a way to prove myself, but if you add more fuel to my fire like this guy did, then you're going to get burned pretty quick," Christian said later. "My blood was boiling. I came out with all that fire inside of me and energy I was waiting to unleash once I stepped on the mound."

Christian faced three players with a combined eleven seasons in the major leagues—Darnell Sweeney, Pete Kozma, and Gaby Guerrero—in the first. He needed just thirteen pitches to strike them all out. Kozma, a former first-round pick, went down in ten seconds on three straight pitches. Overall, Christian needed just two minutes and five seconds to finish the inning.

Afterward, Sweeney told Christian, "You were so nasty, I couldn't even see the ball!"

Those three strikeouts gave us the jolt of energy we needed.

We sailed into the fifth inning, leading 2–1, when things suddenly came undone. Our pitcher, David Moore, just couldn't find the zone. The Monarchs got five sprints (walks) and two hits in the inning while scoring four runs. Although no baseball team would ever concede anything, realistically, it would have been tough to salvage that inning.

Then the tide turned.

After a couple of base hits and an out, that's when our head coach, Eric Byrnes, put himself up as a pinch hitter. He smacked a two-strike RBI single, and when Bill LeRoy came to the plate against Nick Belzer, the Monarchs pitcher, there were still two runners aboard.

Bill was having fun, trying to get the crowd engaged, and clapping both hands above his head, as he does, after taking two balls. Then, he pulled the bat back into position, got his feet set, and delivered a three-run homer to tie the inning and keep us in the overall lead. Bill had never been a power guy. He had had only one home run as a four-year college Banana.

Bill called it one of the best moments of his baseball life. And he said, "If you want to know what Bananaland is all about, clap your hands on a two–oh count, turn around on the pitcher, then hit a three-run homer. That's what we're all about. We can play. But we can also entertain and put on a show."

Our show that day included the ten-foot-tall Stilts coming in to gasps and cheers, then pitching an out. Later, seventy-five-year-old Bill Lee emerged from the stands, where he had been sitting with fans, to get an inning-ending fly ball. We hit high points all night, including Tanner Thomas walking the "yellow carpet" like he was a model during New York Fashion Week. Without breaking character, he declared with a heavy accent that he was wearing "Dolce Banana." Everyone broke into laughter, even the Monarchs players.

The Monarchs got a sixth-inning run to tie it up; then we won it 3–2 in the seventh when Jonny Gomes worked the count full, then took a ball low. In Bananaland, we call that a walk-off walk. Bill LeRoy scored easily from third base.

For me, the whole weekend unfolded at warp speed. There was too much to process. Bottom line: we went into the home park of a legitimately strong pro team and beat them with Banana Ball rules. It worked.

I think Viro put it best. "The Monarchs are just like us, a bunch of guys who remember having so much fun playing ball as kids," Viro said. "We taught them how to play Banana Ball, but we also showed them *why* we do this—for the fans.

"So you saw all these grizzled former major leaguers with big smiles on their faces, interacting with the fans, dancing to 'Hey

Baby' along with us. I hope they take those qualities into their season. They bought in. They had fun. That's a huge win for the Bananas, and it shows us the future of Banana Ball is like a rocket ship."

Kyle Luigs said he had never signed as many autographs as the two nights in Kansas City—and he's been doing this for five years. He was so impressed with the attitude of the Monarchs. I agree. Those guys could've big-timed us or maybe thought it was disrespectful for this crazy team to come onto their field and perform all these antics. But the Monarchs played along beautifully. Monarchs manager Joe Calfapietra, who didn't seem to have much enthusiasm at the beginning, said he felt it was a worthy experience and he loved seeing his ballpark alive with enthusiasm. He told his players to keep an open mind, and they ended up enjoying the games.

Here's the part I really loved. The Monarchs said they had never had more fun playing baseball. That's our mission statement.

Kozma said, "It's hard to watch the Bananas and not smile."

That's so cool coming from a guy who played with the Cardinals, Yankees, Rangers, Tigers, and Athletics. Kozma said he could visualize being a Banana one day.

"I mean, there's an enormous following, and everywhere they go, they sell out," he said. "It's kind of tough to ignore."

The Monarchs used Steven Damico, who played on the 2016 Coastal Carolina NCAA championship team, as a pitcher. He was really into it, clapping his hands and shaking his body to the music when he was on the mound. Afterward, he said, "I'm still shaking from how much fun it was. This was ten times as fun as any baseball game I've ever seen. This is the way baseball should be—fun for the players, the fans, the coaches—even the umpires."

Matt Adams, the Monarchs' best and most recognizable player, said he was skeptical at first, but it didn't take long for him to buy in. Some of the Monarchs got together and agreed to treat it like the WWE's *Monday Night Raw*. Their inner wrestlers came out in a big way.

"It's really a lot of fun," Adams said. "I'm at a loss for words. At first, it seemed out of my comfort zone. But then I was like, 'Hell yeah, let's do this.' It was a blast. How can you be against putting more fun in baseball?"

When the games end, we love to finish with a bang. We had a surprise fireworks show planned, but the wind changed, and the fire marshal said we couldn't do it. We adjusted.

After Jonny Gomes got his walk-off walk and we had beaten the Monarchs, I grabbed the microphone for my usual thank-you messages to everyone. I hadn't planned it at all, but something came over me and I said, "KANSAS CITY! We're coming back next year!!"

The fans went nuts. Emily and the staff said it was the loudest the place had been all weekend. The Monarchs' owners were jumping around in celebration. It was party time.

I joined in and danced harder and longer than ever before. Up on the stadium plaza, I made sure to grab hold of Bill LeRoy when the pep band started our traditional "Stand by Me" finale because of all he had done during the memorable weekend.

"This is your dream, man," Bill said to me.

I corrected him. "Bill, this is our dream. And we're just getting started."

We went upstairs to a suite for a postgame celebration. But the ESPN crew caught me outside for an interview, and my emotions bubbled over. I couldn't help it. I felt such relief and happiness. It probably seemed like I was babbling and repeating myself, but it was such a moment of validation for our organization.

My mind was everywhere. It was on what I'd heard at the Negro Leagues Baseball Museum and the obligation and responsibility I now felt to help revitalize that level of baseball showmanship. It was on all the work and planning that had gone into this weekend with the Monarchs. It was on the fear I'd initially felt about playing another team, whether it would actually work, whether the fans would love our show. And the games couldn't have gone better.

I'm guessing it was about two o'clock in the morning when my dad and I were among the twenty or so people who closed down the party. The hotel was just across a parking lot next to the stadium, and I was definitely ready to get some sleep. I was pretty much emotionally exhausted.

In the morning, we got on the plane heading home. It was Mother's Day.

Kenna and I were sitting in the row ahead of Emily and Mav. I'm always with Kenna. She always wants to take a nap next to Daddy.

We were pulling away from the gate, getting ready to take off, and I turned back to tell Em something through the crack between the seats. She was crying and staring at her phone.

I nearly jumped up, but looked back to ask, "Hey, what's wrong? What's wrong?"

Through her tears and trying not to alarm the kids, Emily said, "Tina just sent me a message. Here, look."

Tina is the biological mother of our youngest kiddo, Addison.

As I read the heartfelt message on Emily's phone, I, too, began to cry.

Tina wrote: "I wanted to make your Mother's Day special."

Tina asked us to adopt Addison.

She wanted her daughter to have the best possible life. There were probably no words to express her pain, especially when faced with such an emotional decision, but she put her daughter's welfare above all else.

As Tina wrote: "I would be honored and forever grateful for you guys to adopt her. The sooner, the better, for her sake. I truly hope this can be a beautiful thing. I hope you have a wonderful Mother's Day."

We were overwhelmed.

Sometimes in life, a whole period of time flashes right before your eyes in just a few seconds. This was one of those moments.

When we first started attending foster care information sessions in 2019, we were told directly, "This is not how you build your forever family. Kids will come and go from your home and you have to be comfortable with the lack of permanency."

The goal of foster care is to walk alongside children and families when they need support, and help them reunify with their biological family. We were warned by many and we knew—it would hurt to fall in love with a child, raise them, and send them home.

But we kept coming back to a few things:

How do we worry about our potential heartache when there's a little kid out there who is in a lot more pain? Emily and I had each other, a huge support system, access to resources . . . so many things that could help us through our potential future. But these kids? They didn't ask to be in this situation. They couldn't be with their parents or in their home anymore. Regardless of "how bad" a situation is, kids usually want to be home with the people they know. Leaving that space and their family is traumatic.

What if we were able to offer stability and a foundation for these kids that would help them wherever they went in life? That could be the goal—get them healthier, show them love, teach them to swim, all of it. Those would be things they could have long after they left our home. We were just a safe landing pad.

We knew we needed to open our home and share what we had. So we jumped in.

Society doesn't talk enough about the kids in foster care, and it's even more rare that we talk about the rest of the family.

Fortunately, we had devoured information in the years leading up to our getting licensed and we knew we should treat our kiddos' families with respect. The situations they are coming out of are often generational problems, and it's easy to understand how they fell into whatever bad spot they were in. Maybe not excusable, but understandable.

We began a beautiful relationship with Addison's mom from the very start. Her story is hers to tell, not mine, so I'll keep it generic. She wasn't able to care for Addison after birth, and at six days old, Addie was placed in our care from the NICU. When she was eight days old, we all attended her first doctors' appointment together. The doctors asked questions and Tina answered some that only she could answer, and we did the same. It was our first real sense of shared parenting. Over the months that followed, we saw one another multiple times a week as Tina worked her case plan to get Addie back. There were definitely ups and downs, but we were all always kind and respectful to one another and we usually felt like a team.

So now here we were, heading home from Kansas City. Addison was seven months old and hadn't been able to travel out of state with us for this trip because of some foster care regulations. That's when we received Tina's message.

And our deepest emotions were brought to the surface.

Tina's message was the most selfless decision. She told us she was going to voluntarily terminate her rights, so Addie didn't need to be dragged through the court system for years. Tina didn't anticipate her lifestyle changing for a while and she wanted Addie to settle into our loving family and be adopted by us before she was old enough to truly understand the pain of the whole situation.

Her message was the most beautiful, mature, thoughtful thing I've ever read. And she wanted to send it to Em as a gift on Mother's Day. In the midst of her despair, she was thinking about others. How incredible was that?

It was another lesson for me. We have no idea what someone is going through or what kind of person they are. Before judging by appearance or situation, remember that we might not be able to fathom the things they are going through.

During this period of my life, I often reflected on my mother and her problems. Getting involved in the foster care world and out of my little comfortable-life bubble helped me to gain a lot of perspective. I started feeling a lot of peace and forgiveness toward my mom during this time.

To this day, we have a great relationship with Tina and Addison's grandparents. We share pictures and stories. We're able to get health information from them, and they visit for holidays and birthdays. Addie will always know how courageous her birth mom was and how much she loved her to be able to make that decision.

I'll never forget what I saw while looking through the crack between those two airplane seats. Emily crying with happy tears, of course. But also sad tears for Tina and Addison and the rest of their family. We didn't go into fostering seeking a route for adoption, yet here we were. And wow, was it emotional!

Adoption can be a wonderful thing. But it always, always comes from something that was broken.

People see the craziness of our games, the sellout crowds, the over-the-top social media. There's a deeper picture to all of this. We're all on this mission to bring people together and create unbelievable joy.

I don't remember much of the plane ride to Kansas City, but I do remember everything about the flight back. And we couldn't wait to get home to our little girl. Tina's incredible decision brought everything full circle.

What we do is always about family.

Chapter Twenty

The Future

After our summer college team won the 2022 Coastal Plain League (CPL) championship—the third title for our summer-league club—we made a decision that jump-started our future.

We decided to leave the CPL to become a full-time Banana Ball team. We wanted to tour the United States and the whole world on our schedule.

It's funny how people react to change. It was clearly the most fans-first decision we've ever made with the Bananas. When we played in the CPL opposing parks, we couldn't put on our normal show because we don't control that. For CPL games in Savannah, we greet fans at the gate and celebrate with them afterward. On the road for CPL games, we can only just show up and play. Since the league is a nine-inning, conventional baseball operation, there really is no way to implement Banana Ball.

When fans came from far and wide to see us play summer ball on the road, they usually left disappointed. They wanted to know: Where are the Savannah Bananas we've heard so much about? It was completely different from the World Tour, when

it was Banana Ball rules and the Bananas against the Party
Animals.

Well, now the fans get the Bananas and full-fledged Banana
Ball all the time. I call that a victory. Still, there's always a group
that thinks the worst, as if we have devious intentions. It's just
not true. We always intend to keep Savannah as our home base
and the site for games. By expanding to a full Banana Ball tour,
we're giving more fans the opportunity to experience what they
enjoy the most. When we took over the Savannah franchise,
everyone told us we were doomed to fail. It's not that long ago
that nobody would return our phone calls when we sought sponsors and ticket sales.

But Savannah is our heritage. Jeff Bezos, Amazon's founder,
once said, "You have to be willing to be misunderstood." I understand that completely. We've been misunderstood by some since
the day we arrived. But it's how you respond to criticism that
matters the most.

When we announced our decision to go all-in on Banana Ball,
the response was overwhelmingly positive. But we also received
a good amount of harsh criticism about the decision. We'd gone
through some of this before. When we first came to Savannah,
we were criticized for being a college summer team and not a
professional team. Months later, we were criticized for naming
the team the Savannah Bananas.

But criticism of our decision to fully embrace Banana Ball
probably hurt the most because Emily and I and our entire team
worked hard for seven years to build the trust of our fans. We
know that not everyone truly knows us, our hearts, our vision,
and the whole story. And we know change is hard, and not everyone will agree with every decision we make. But we lost some of
that trust.

It still hurts.

Here's a sampling of the social media reaction:

I know Jesse is a marketing genius who could probably sell ice to an Eskimo, but I hope this traveling circus falls flat on its face. Sure, it's cute and kitschy, but I'll bet the novelty will wear off soon. What a mockery.

Such a sad choice. It was definitely not a fan based decision. Take Savannah out of your name. Jesse's Joke sounds about right.

I guess the yellow top hat was in preparation for the full blown circus. I hope the attendance drops, then the Bananas will realize this is really an epic fail. Tickets will not be hard to get now!

Jesse and the team have sold out. Money over true fans.

The key for Emily and me is to reframe the criticism. I always say, "If you are not getting criticized, you are playing it too safe." Criticism is never the goal, but anyone who stands for something and goes all-in on what they believe will probably be criticized.

We know we are not for everyone. If you try to be everything to everyone, you won't be anything to anyone. We are not for most baseball purists. We are for people who want to have fun.

Our goal with expanding Banana Ball was to give more fans the opportunity to go bananas. We added more games and more opponents, to be in front of more fans on an annual basis. It gave us the opportunity to play all over the world at any time and schedule games whenever we want in Savannah, not just in the hottest months. It also allows us to play what we believe is the most entertaining form of baseball.

Belief is a powerful force. When you believe in your vision and your dreams, anything is possible. The greatest visionaries see things others can't see. At minimum, I see something that provides joy and fun to millions of people. The fans are who we work for. We won't stop until we deliver the best possible fan experience and the greatest show in sports. You've got to stand for something and I believe our approach has earned us a more loyal fan base than we ever could've expected.

That's something we'll never ignore even as our fan base expands.

The Bananas on national TV? How a-peel-ing! The ESPN series came together in a way that wasn't expected. First, one of the ESPN writers came to do a story on us early in 2021. It got a great response, and ESPN's TV side wanted to follow up. They hired David Beilinson and RUMUR, an independent film studio, to produce a seven-minute feature that appeared on *Sports-Center*. This was August 2021, and the social media response was huge.

We literally had a *SportsCenter* anchor who said going to a Savannah Bananas game was on her bucket list.

At that point, about thirty-five production companies had reached out to us about a documentary series. I knew I wanted to do it with David. So he pitched ESPN, but they weren't interested. Then I got involved for one more pitch, but they basically told me, "We've never done anything like this. No offense, Jesse, but you're not Tom Brady, you're not Michael Jordan, you're not Derek Jeter."

I said, "No, I'm not. But we can give you a show that's different than anything you've ever seen."

For the next three months, I sent personal videos to the head
people at ESPN. I told them, "We've had doubters since we came
to Savannah. But if you believe in us, it's going to work." I sent
them something almost weekly.

In January 2022, I was with Emily when David texted me,
"Boom!"

I was like, "What?"

David texted: "They just said yes." ESPN was going to green-
light a TV show on the Savannah Bananas and our World Tour.

Our momentum exploded after that. The *Today* show, HBO
Real Sports, *CBS Sunday Morning* . . . they all came to Savannah.
So I went to ESPN programming and said, "Hey, let's show a
game." They were skeptical. So we invested in it, where there was
no significant cost for them. Our team worked tirelessly for weeks
to get it done in Bananas fashion. We didn't make a dollar of
profit. Everything ESPN provided was put right back into the
production, so the fans could get a quality product. The social
media buzz alone made it worth the cost.

Attention beats marketing 1,000 percent of the time. That's
what I believe. We don't have a marketing plan. We have an attention plan. We believe Banana Ball will continue to grow with
this approach. We're not putting a ceiling on it because we're not
sure how big it can get.

Still, people believe what they want to believe. I've heard it
said that if Jesse Cole were offered $5 million to become general
manager or president of the Boston Red Sox, he'd leave so fast
that there would be skid marks. But they could offer me $100
million and I wouldn't take it.

I go back to something Walt Disney said. *Money doesn't excite me. My ideas excite me.* Money will never entice me to do anything. I want to do things that matter or things that are fun. I want to be creative and different. In the front offices of most major sports teams, there are too many cooks in the kitchen and rolls of red tape, making it too tough to exercise creativity. The reality is I couldn't make a big enough impact because ideas get watered-down. I don't *ever* want to water *anything* down.

There will be conversations about another baseball league in the future. I feel certain about that. It's happened with golf, with football. Will it be a Banana Ball league? I mean, I could visualize it, but MLB is one-hundred-plus years old. Here's a more likely scenario: I think just like the NBA, which evolved in part because of the Harlem Globetrotters, MLB will be forced to evolve as well.

I think MLB executives are some of the brightest people in sports. People like that generally learn from other organizations and approaches, especially if they're disruptive in their own industry. MLB has noticed that we sell out every game and have a long waiting list for tickets. It sees our social media presence and knows that's a wave of the future. Our fans are loyal, and they spread our message, so undoubtedly MLB would like to tap into that.

We're playing a different game. If MLB ultimately takes some things from our game and our experiences, I think that's a win for everyone.

Our organization started with a blank slate in 2016 when we knew the game had to change. We had no preconceived notions. Our principle was incredibly simple: What parts of a baseball game are long, slow, and boring? How do we do the opposite? We saw that fans were leaving early every single night—a fact we didn't discover because of a survey but because we watched them—so a two-hour time limit was a big push. Then it was coming up with other ways to speed the game along and keep searching for things fans had never seen on a baseball field. We never stopped observing what our fans said they wanted. They wanted entertainment, speed, and convenience.

MLB has rules, regulations, and committees. The greatest thing about the Savannah Bananas is we can play by our own rules. We don't have a governing body other than our own imagination. We can have cameras on anybody at any time. We can put cameras inside baseballs or inside bats. We can have everyone miked up at the same time. We can have pitchers talking on the broadcast, telling fans what pitch they're going to throw and why. Because of MLB's structure, it needs approval and consensus before it moves forward on almost anything.

We train our players in the skills that are entertaining and exciting. We want outfielders who can catch a ball and do a split. We want the shortstop to field a grounder and flip the ball behind his back to the second baseman for the force-out.

The Bananas will continue to attract a higher caliber of player—the fan following and social media exposure are huge incentives—and they will be able to show the world their unique tricks and talents. I think we're at the point where playing for the Bananas will have a greater appeal for some players instead of, say, having a "cup of coffee" with any MLB team. That's because of our organization's enormous exposure, and its freedom on style of play, and its ability to change the game.

We went from our one-city, two-night World Tour (Mobile) in 2021 to seven cities in 2022. Each game sold out. The 2023 World Tour has upped the ante with ten-thousand-seat stadiums and Triple A parks. MLB stadiums are next.

One of Michael Jackson's biggest fears was overexposure, and once in a while, he would disappear for a couple of years. I'm not worried about overexposure because I know there are many people in the world who haven't heard of Banana Ball yet.

Even with a nine-inning Coastal Plain League game, where we couldn't perform most of our antics, we had people saying they had never seen anything like this in their life and it was so fun. Wait until the full-fledged Banana Ball really hits its stride. I still think we have a huge canvas to work with.

The trick is going to be logistics. People always try to compare us to MLB. The better comparison might be the WWE, the Grateful Dead, Cirque du Soleil—the touring acts.

The Grateful Dead had only one Top 40 single in several decades, but became one of the highest-grossing American touring acts. They assembled a loyal group of fans—the "Deadheads"—and they built a business model on touring. They allowed fans to tape and share the music, so following the band on tour became a huge thing. The band handled ticketing and eliminated the middleman to deal directly with their fans.

They stayed relevant by doing what their fans wanted. The Bananas try to do the same thing. My biggest fear is becoming irrelevant, so I look at companies and entertainment acts that have stood the test of time.

We're not sure on the timetable for this, but we'd like to build a "Bananaland" or "Banana World" complex, where fans can make a pilgrimage to enjoy our brand of baseball. I see it as a place that brings people together through the joy and fun of Banana Ball. It will be "the Most Fun Ballpark in the World." People will come every day, whether we're putting on a show or not, and feel something special.

Imagine a banana grove going across the whole stadium. Imagine zip lines across the whole field. Imagine the world's largest banana lighthouse, a two-hundred-foot-tall banana that visitors can climb up to see all of Savannah. Imagine a train traveling around the field, tree houses, Airbnbs, bungalows and breweries, a banana beach with a pool and sand. Imagine a banana sweets shop and bakery. Imagine Club 26, the best seats in the house located twenty-six feet from home plate, with a speakeasy located beneath it. We'll call it Club 26 because Grayson Stadium was built in 1926.

Looking for a cool vacation idea? Welcome to Banana Cruises. Let's get three thousand of your closest friends, along with the Bananas players, and have the time of our lives. Every other day, we'll stop at an island, disembark, and play a Banana Ball game. We'll be back on the boat for the after-party and to get some sleep as we head for our next destination.

To keep advancing our game, we'll have Banana Ball Little Leagues, where kids will grow up learning how to play fast and have fun. One day, we might even have the Banana Ball Little League World Series.

The truth is, there's always a better idea, a new way to look at things, or an event that can really shake things up. Attention beats marketing—1,000 percent of the time.

Every Monday, our staff gets together and we kick around ideas in our OTT (Over-The-Top) sessions. Then we write them down and rehearse them. We perform something new every single week. That's what we want. Every single week, we want ideas on things that have never been seen before on a baseball field.

Even if fans have seen the Savannah Bananas before, they know that they will see something new and exciting the next time.

With the Bananas, we are limited only by our imagination. As they say, teamwork makes the dream work. Dreams keep people highly motivated. Dreams put a smile on people's faces when they wake up in the morning.

There's one particular dream that makes me super excited.

Those who follow baseball, even if it's just a little bit, know about Fenway Park, the oldest active ballpark in the major leagues. It's cramped. Parking is difficult. Some fans might have to sit behind a post, obstructing their view. The seats are not plush. And it's one of the most beautiful places I've ever seen.

One day, the Bananas will be playing at major-league ballparks—and selling them out. Fenway Park, where I saw dozens and dozens of Red Sox games as a kid, wants to be the first MLB stadium to host a Banana Ball game.

When I was five years old, I had the opportunity to be a Red Sox batboy. I still have a picture of me with Lee Smith, a Red Sox relief pitcher who is now in the Baseball Hall of Fame.

When I was twenty, I pitched at Fenway when I played in the Cranberry Baseball League All-Star Game during an amateur independent league season. It was so real to me—the sights, the sounds, the smells—and pretty much mesmerizing.

The odds of *any* kid reaching the major leagues is astronomical. I thought it was my destiny. Me at Fenway making my major-league debut. I would look up in the stands and see my dad beaming proudly.

Then I got hurt.

Now there's a new dream.

At a typical game in Savannah, we pack in about four thousand fans, and an additional twenty-five million people watch our videos.

And I have written this down—2025: Play live in front of one million fans! That would be more than any NFL, NBA, or NHL team in one season. It's even more than some MLB teams draw in an entire season, over their eighty-one home games.

So what's the dream? We will sell out major-league stadiums. We will sell out Fenway Park. That might sound cocky or confident, but I know how the Bananas make people feel. It's not just a baseball team. It's a grassroots movement. I feel our biggest goals can and will happen because we have a team of talented people.

Dreams should be big. It's like my dad used to say, "Swing hard in case you hit it." Well, we were swinging hard in the middle of our 2022 World Tour when the call came from Tim Zue, chief financial officer of the Boston Red Sox.

"We've been following what the Bananas are doing and we're fascinated," Tim told me. "What do you think about playing at Fenway Park?"

Other MLB teams have stepped up—we'd heard from the Diamondbacks, Giants, Royals, Nationals, Marlins, and Braves by the summer of 2022—so it's clear that will be part of our future when we are ready. People thought that baseball executives would hate us and want nothing to do with us, but that hasn't been the case. In the short term, we're working on growing our product and our brand. In the long term, I expect us to work together. It gives validity to the Bananas if we partner with MLB. People throughout baseball are taking notes and saying, "Baseball can be more fun. It can be like this."

I think it's all on the table.

Bananas at the All-Star Game.
Bananas at the College World Series.
Bananas at the Little League World Series.

Bananas at the *Field of Dreams* cornfield ballpark.

Bananas at the Baseball Hall of Fame.

How large we grow—and how fast we grow—will be determined by one thing: what the fans want. We are "Fans First"—then, now, and always.

"When Jesse was born, my hopes and thoughts were that he would love baseball," my dad said. "Our trips to Fenway were frequent. The games were enjoyable. But I could also watch them through Jesse's eyes as he fell in love with baseball.

"I love antiques. Fenway Park is a masterpiece. I just love watching games there. I love to walk through Kenmore Square and see how the whole crowd comes through the city to get to the park. To see the Bananas at Fenway Park? I'm not sure I have the words for that."

It probably starts with pie-in-the-sky wishful thinking. Then maybe some hope, followed by a potential opportunity that happens ahead of the timetable. It all leads to reality.

Dreams are based on memories, but they are also creations, so the brushstrokes aren't limited to just logical things. Things don't even have to make sense. It's a nightly adventure.

So I will dream.

I dream I am at Fenway Park, by myself in the locker room because I need time to settle my emotions. The warm-ups are underway, and I can hear the marching band's music and the crowd's muffled roar. Banana Ball has arrived in Boston.

My dad turns to me and says, "You ready? It's showtime."

I'm awestruck, somewhere in that murky world between

dreams and reality. Fenway Park is packed, and all the fans are wearing our canary yellow gear.

I study every corner—from the Green Monster to the Pesky Pole to up in the press box. My dad is with Emily in the dugout, and both are fighting back tears. My friends and family are there in the stands. I'm back on the field, introducing the greatest show in sports, feeling just like I did when the game first grabbed ahold of me. I always say it's not your grandpa's pastime, but the cool thing is we're in a ballpark that your grandpa probably loved. I look around, and I'm the last to know: Every Bananas player is applauding, even the Party Animals. And those fans? They made all of this happen.

It's like my whole life passes before my eyes—everything and everyone I care about, converging in a moment that is so perfect, it's almost too good for a dream.

Every day with the Bananas, I feel like a kid again. I truly feel like it's just the beginning. I look forward to every day and don't want this feeling to end.

That's what happens when you're living your dream.

Deep breath. It's time for the show. I'm not even nervous. I don't think I've felt more comfortable or more happy. I'm at home.

As I said at the beginning, this is a love story.

Epilogue

At some point, I believe the Savannah Bananas will have one billion fans and we will be recognized as the world's largest sports and entertainment company.

That's an ambitious goal. It's also a wonderful dream.

But it carries a great responsibility.

Now more than ever, I feel a tremendous duty to our fans, especially those who have been with us since the beginning, as well as to the people on our team, the players who make it happen, some of the most creative and talented athletes you'll ever find.

We have to keep innovating, creating, and inventing on the fans' behalf. We have to keep the Bananas fresh. While I'm alive, I will never let the Bananas go rotten or forget why we do what we do and whom we serve.

My hope is that many years after I'm gone, the Bananas remain, continuing to put the fans first with everything. We must continue to dream big and reimagine what is possible, both with Banana Ball and the fan experience.

We always listen to our fans. Remember how we set up our thirty-three-city World Tour in 2023?

We held a live draft reveal on the Internet so we could build the suspense. We had thirty thousand unique viewers who wanted to see the cities that had been selected. About eight o'clock that night, more than fifty-five thousand people went to our website at the same moment and tried to buy tickets.

It was the most traffic we had ever seen on our website—and we weren't even playing a game. We've hit a nerve, and now it's our responsibility to keep finding the right mix of sports and entertainment to delight the fans and keep them coming back.

We love competitiveness in sports, but we also love story lines. Roone Arledge, the former head of ABC Sports, was brilliant at that. He got you to care about the Olympics. You were riveted by the story of a young woman from Russia, how her career began, what obstacles she had overcome to win a gold medal. You had never even heard of this athlete. But when Roone Arledge humanized an athlete and told you a story, you couldn't look away. He made you care.

We want to put you behind the scenes with our players and keep them accessible. Fans crave creative and compelling storytelling, and that will always be one of our biggest missions with the Bananas.

Sometimes, you can get too big and you lose sight of the qualities that made you successful in the first place. I promise you this: That will never happen with the Bananas. We've never made one decision based on money, and we're not going to start now, no matter how big we get (Banana Ball on the moon!).

As much as things have changed, one thing never will:

Fans First. Entertain Always.

Thank you for being the driving force behind our journey. You are the reason for our success. Banana Nation, we've only just begun!

Jesse Cole
Savannah, Georgia

Acknowledgments

THANK YOU.

As we finish this book, I am overcome with gratitude for everyone who made this happen.

Since starting the Savannah Bananas with Emily, I've had big dreams for this team. But never, in my wildest dreams, did I ever envision creating a new game of baseball that would make such an impact around the world.

The creation of Banana Ball and this book are the results of amazing people coming together to put the fans first and challenge the way things were done in the past.

For the numerous people who played a role in this book, your support along the way is what made it come to fruition.

First, to Banana Nation. You've been there for it all. While at first many of you were understandably skeptical about this new team named after a fruit (I don't blame you), since coming out of that first game, you've embraced this team and everything we stand for.

With every rule change and decision for Banana Ball, we thought of you and experimented on your behalf. The same is true with this book. Our mission is *Fans First. Entertain Always*, and our goal was to put you first and make this book as entertaining as possible while telling the in-depth story of how Banana Ball came to be.

Next, the biggest Bananas fans, our team members. To our entire full-time staff, part-time staff, players, coaches, and cast, who make the magic happen daily in Savannah and all over the world on our Banana Ball tour, thank you for your tireless dedication to the fans. You bring the joy and the fun to the fans and to everyone in the office. You make me truly proud of what we've built and the impact we are making. I'm grateful to be doing it alongside each of you.

With the book alone, the biggest thank-you must go to Don Yaeger. For years, I admired you from afar as a fan of your writing and storytelling. After we first spoke, I looked up to you even more. To see you believe in me, this book, and our Banana Ball movement means more than you know. You immersed yourself in Bananaland and put your heart into this project. From the beginning it was obvious how much you cared about telling this story and making me and Banana Nation proud. You've done that and so much more, my friend.

To Joey Johnston, for your amazing research and interviews to help tell our story. From the first tryout through the end of the tour, you were there and became a huge part of the team. I am honored to call you a Banana.

For the team at Dutton who believed in this project and worked with me on this book for over a year. Specifically, John Parsley for being such a big supporter and being open to doing things differently with this book.

To my dad, even today, I'm still just that five-year-old kid coming to bat and swinging hard, trying to make you proud. Dad, you've encouraged me every step of the way and pushed me to work hard and stay positive with everything I do. I love you, Dad, and I hope I made you proud with this book.

To my kids, thank you for the laughter, the fun, and the joy you bring to our lives. You've made me think about everything we can do to make the Bananas experience fun for adults and kids. Many of the rules of Banana Ball and the fun parts of our show were created with you in mind! Daily, I continue to try to create something you'd love that we can experience together.

Finally, my wife, Emily. After the first draft of this book was complete, Emily dropped everything and booked a flight to meet with Don and spend an entire day editing the book. Her dedication and care for me, our family, and our team are simply unbelievable. She's been the rock for me and our family since the first day I met her. When I proposed on the field in front of a sold-out crowd and said, "Will you make me the luckiest man in the world?" I am so grateful her answer was yes to that crazy guy in a yellow tuxedo. I still feel like I'm the luckiest guy today—even more so than I did back then.

This has been quite the journey for Emily and me and our team, but we know we are just getting started. We often say in the office that we are still in the first inning, and I believe that is true.

Our goal with the Bananas is to continue to make baseball fun and bring people together through the joy of Banana Ball. We have a strong vision for Banana Ball and plan to spread more Fans First fun all over the world in the years to come.

So, for allowing us to share our story and supporting us while we chase these dreams, we thank you from the bottom of our hearts.

We love you, Banana Nation. Thanks again for everything and keep going, Bananas!

About the Author

Jesse Cole is the founder of Fans First Entertainment and owner of the Savannah Bananas. He has been featured on more than 1,000 podcasts and delivers keynote speeches all over the world. He lives in North Carolina and Georgia with his wife, son, and two daughters. He owns seven yellow tuxedos.

Don Yaeger has authored more than thirty books, including eleven *New York Times* bestsellers. He was a longtime associate editor at *Sports Illustrated* and is the host of the highly acclaimed Corporate Competitor Podcast. He lives in Tallahassee, Florida, with his wife, son, and daughter. His tux is boring and black.